CLEATS OR TOE SHOES?

"I can't believe you're running out on the team!" Breezy yelled. "It sounds to me as if you've already made your choice!"

Crystal paused and started to walk back toward Breezy. Then she stopped. Madame would be really mad if she was any later than she already was for ballet. She had to run if she was going to make it in time.

"Breezy . . ." she began.

"Fine, C.J.!" Breezy said loudly, turning back to the rest of the Parrots. "Go off to your little dance class. See if I care. We'll just make do with one less player. No big deal."

Crystal felt tears welling up in the corners of her eyes. Why couldn't Breezy understand that Madame, everyone at the ballet academy, and her family were all counting on her to be in this recital? She couldn't let them down. But she was already really late . . .

THE PINK PARROTS

FIELDER'S CHOICE

Created by Lucy Ellis

By B. B. Calhoun

A *SPORTS ILLUSTRATED FOR KIDS* BOOK

Created by Lucy Ellis
Written by B. B. Calhoun
Cover art by Gary Glover
Cover design by Pegi Goodman
Interior line art by Jane Davila
Produced by Angel Entertainment, Inc.

SPORTS ILLUSTRATED FOR KIDS Books is a joint imprint of Little, Brown and Company and Warner Juvenile Books.

Printed in the United States of America

First Printing: May 1991
10 9 8 7 6 5 4 3 2 1

Published simultaneously in Canada by Little, Brown & Company (Canada) Limited

Library of Congress Cataloging-in-Publication Data

Calhoun, B. B., 1961-
Fielder's choice / B.B. Calhoun ; created by Lucy Ellis.
p. cm. — (The Pink parrots ; #4)
"A Sports illustrated for kids book."
Summary: When twelve-year-old Crystal Joseph is chosen to dance the lead in "Sleeping Beauty" she worries about losing her friends and her position as first baseman for the Pink Parrots.
ISBN 0-316-12447-8
[1. Dancing — Fiction 2. Baseball — Fiction. 3. Sex role — Fiction.]
I. Ellis, Lucy. II. Title. III. Series.
PZ7.C12744Fi 1991
[Fic] — dc20 90-55743
CIP
AC

This book is available in hardcover library binding from: Lerner Publications Company, 241 First Avenue North, Minneapolis, Minnesota 55401
1-800-328-4929
ISBN: 0-8225-3113-5

1

"There's no way you're going to win with the bases loaded and Hammerin' Hank at bat," Matt Ryan said to Crystal Joseph, the Pink Parrots first baseman. Matt took a lead off the bag. "No way at all," he repeated, moving closer to her.

Crystal ignored him and wiped the sweat off her forehead as she squinted at the batter. Hammerin' Hank Farber stepped out of the batter's box and swung his bat around a few times.

Crystal glanced at Breezy Hawk, the pitcher and captain of the Pink Parrots. Breezy stood on the mound with her glove tucked under her right arm, rubbing the ball between her hands. Then she took off her cap, and pushed aside the stray dirty blonde hairs that had escaped from her ponytail before pulling her cap back firmly onto her head. Breezy slowly put on her glove, giving Hammerin' Hank a long, hard look as he stepped back into the batter's box. Crystal was glad that she wasn't in his shoes. She knew that Breezy had this really intimidating way of looking at a batter. Crystal thought that Breezy was an incredible baseball player.

The Parrots were playing Burger Bonanza. It was the bottom of the sixth and final inning and the score was 9-6, in the Parrots' favor. But the bases were loaded and Hank Farber wasn't called Hammerin' Hank for nothing.

"Nobatter, nobatter, nobatter," Kim Yardley chanted as Breezy went into her windup. Kim, the Parrots shortstop, was one of the best shortstops in the Eastern Maryland Baseball League (Emblem) and was almost as competitive as her best friend, Breezy. Crystal couldn't believe how single-minded both of them could be about baseball sometimes — especially Breezy.

Baseball was everything to Breezy. She practically lived and breathed the game. In fact, she had formed the Pink Parrots, the only all-girls team in Emblem, out of frustration that girls didn't get to play as much as boys. Crystal admired Breezy a lot; she was actually the reason that Crystal had joined the Parrots in the first place. Sometimes, she wished she had her friend's dedication.

Breezy's first pitch rocketed right up the middle of the plate. Hammerin' Hank swung a little late but still caught a piece of the ball. He scooped it a bit, though, and the ball popped straight up and went over the backstop behind him.

"Strike one," the umpire yelled.

Crystal could tell that Breezy was really concentrating. She went into her windup almost as soon as she got the ball back from Terry DiSunno, the Parrots catcher. Breezy blasted another fastball across the plate, nicking the outside corner. It could have been an instant replay for Hammerin' Hank. He popped it up and over the backstop again.

"You've got two, girl!" someone called from the Pink Parrots dugout. "Bear down and strike him out!"

Crystal glanced over at Rose Ann DiMona, the Parrots coach and sponsor. Ro, who owned the Pink Parrot Beauty salon, was wearing bright pink high-top sneakers and purple and pink polka-dotted leggings under her Pink Parrots uniform shirt. She was pacing the dugout, her jaw working up and down as she chewed furiously on a piece of gum.

Breezy nodded at the coach and quickly went into her windup. She rifled a pitch down the center of the plate. Hank swung a little early, but the bat made solid contact with the ball. He sent a mammoth shot out toward leftfield. Crystal held her breath as the ball kept rising and rising toward home run territory. She slowly exhaled as the shot drifted two feet over the foul line just short of the wall.

Matt turned back to Crystal. "Hank always hits a foul before he sends one out," he said, smirking. "Just wait."

Crystal ignored him again. She knew he was just trying to get a reaction. If she didn't say anything, it would probably discourage him from continuing. And Crystal also knew that Matt might be right — before every game, Crystal studied the stats of the team they would be playing. Hank Farber had won games for Burger Bonanza with late-inning fireworks before. That didn't mean that it had to happen this time. He was hitting against Breezy, after all. And she was one of the best pitchers in the league.

The Parrots had played a good game, at least until this last inning. The Burger Bonanza runners had loaded the bases on a couple of base hits and an error.

Crystal felt like holding her breath as she watched Breezy shake off Terry's first two signals. Finally, Breezy nodded and went into her windup.

Crystal didn't know what Hammerin' Hank was expecting but it definitely was not the sinker that dropped at least six inches right in front of him.

He chipped wildly at the ball and sent a weak grounder right toward Crystal. She didn't even think; she just reacted. She bent down, expertly scooped up the ball, and leaped toward first base. Beating Hank to the bag, Crystal quickly pivoted and saw Matt sprinting toward second. Within a nanosecond, she had rifled the ball to Julie McKay at second. Matt must have seen Julie catch the ball, because he stopped in his tracks and turned back toward first. Julie zinged the ball back to Crystal. Crystal grabbed the ball and moved toward second and the approaching runner. Then Matt changed directions again.

"You got him in a run-down!" Breezy yelled.

"It's a pickle!" Kim added excitedly.

Crystal quickly threw the ball to Julie and moved closer to second base. Matt turned around and ran back toward first. Crystal had had enough of this. It was time to make the tag. When Julie flipped the ball back to Crystal, she was ready. Crystal caught Julie's throw and chased Matt with the ball. He twisted and turned trying to get to second base safely before Crystal tagged him out. She stayed on him, though. He faked right, pulling Crystal with him and then quickly dashed left, stepped outside the basepath, and then headed for the bag.

"Back, Crystal!" Julie ordered.

Crystal just stopped and held onto the ball as Matt sprinted to second. He stood on the bag, grinning at Crystal, his chest heaving.

"Got you!" he called out.

"Why didn't you throw it back to me?" Julie demanded.

"But . . ." Crystal began, protesting.

"Crystal, we could have gotten him out!" Julie exclaimed, cutting her off.

Crystal looked at Julie helplessly and then turned to the umpire. He started crossing his arms in front of his body as if Matt were safe. But Crystal knew otherwise.

"He ran out of the basepath," Crystal said loudly.

The umpire froze mid-motion. For a second, the whole field was silent.

"You're out of there!" the umpire finally yelled, jerking his thumb at Matt and motioning toward the sidelines.

Crystal gave a little jump. That was three outs. And even though the runners on second and third had scored, the Parrots had won 9-8. Crystal was careful not to look at Matt, who had sat down on second base. She was so happy and she knew that it showed on her face. She didn't want Matt to think she was gloating, though.

Crystal grinned when she heard Ro whoop in the dugout. It was great having such an enthusiastic coach.

"Way to go!" Terry yelled, throwing her catcher's mitt in the air and trotting out toward Crystal. When Terry got to Crystal, she gave her a quick pat on the back and then turned to look behind her.

"What are you doing, Jazz?" Terry asked in astonishment. She raised her eyebrows at Crystal.

Out in rightfield, Jasmine Jaffe, or Jazz, as she was called by almost everyone, was doing cartwheels and aerials. Her hat had fallen off and her long, blonde hair was flying all over the place.

Crystal laughed as Terry, shaking her head at Jazz, walked over to the dugout.

"When you're finished, Jazz . . ." Terry called out over her shoulder.

Suddenly, Breezy and Kim practically jumped on Crystal. Breezy patted her back in congratulation.

"Hey, C.J.!" Breezy exclaimed, grinning. She wiped the sweat off her forehead with the back of her hand.

"Great play! You chased him out of the basepath, didn't you? How'd you know to do that when you've got someone in a pickle?"

"I read about it last night," Crystal admitted with a smile. She knew that Breezy thought it was incredible that anyone could learn how to play baseball from reading a book. Crystal had just started playing the game that season and didn't really know much about it at all. She hadn't even watched a game on television before joining the Pink Parrots. But Crystal figured that she could learn about baseball the same way she had learned about whales, the solar system, and all the other things she was interested in — from books.

"That's out of hand, C.J.," Breezy replied, shaking her head in mock astonishment. "I really don't know how you do it."

Crystal shrugged. "I thought it might come in handy," she explained. She didn't really know what Breezy was talking about. Reading a book was easy. Crystal didn't see what the big deal was. She thought it was probably weird to Breezy because everything about baseball just came naturally to her. What use did Breezy have for a book about the sport?

"Well, you were definitely right about *that* play!" Kim said, laughing.

Breezy threw her arm around Crystal's shoulders and they walked with Kim over to the dugout, where the rest of the team was waiting to start the team cheer.

"All right, birds!" Ro congratulated them. "Way to make a clutch play, Crystal!"

Crystal could feel her face getting warm. It felt great to do a good job on the field, but she found it hard to accept the congratulations. After all, everyone on the team was responsible for the victory, not just Crystal.

"Seriously, C.J.," Breezy added. "You really saved the game with that one. Are you going to be joining the Baltimore Orioles soon, or what?"

Everyone laughed.

"Sorry I yelled at you," Julie apologized. "I should have realized that you knew what you were doing. You always do."

"That's okay," Crystal replied honestly. She knew that tempers often ran high during a game. Everyone wanted to win so much that sometimes little mistakes got blown way out of proportion. Besides, if Matt had been safe, then Julie would have been right to wonder why Crystal hadn't thrown the ball back.

"Well, you and Sarah pitched a great game," Crystal continued, changing the subject. She didn't like to talk about herself. It was enough that *she* knew she had done a good job. Broadcasting it to everyone else was not important to her. In fact, if anything, it was kind of embarrassing.

"Thanks," Breezy said. "But I did get kind of sloppy in the last inning. I can't believe I gave up two hits."

"It even happens to Nolan Ryan," Kim teased. "You

can't be perfect on every single pitch, you know."

"Everyone would be pitching no-hitters then," Crystal added. Sometimes she thought Breezy was too hard on herself. But Crystal knew that baseball was just about the most important thing in life to Breezy and besides, she could kind of understand it, herself. The more she played, the more she realized that baseball was really important to her, too.

2

Crystal practically flew home. When things went right in a baseball game, it made her feel good in a way nothing else ever had. As she walked down Elm Avenue, she was so happy that she leapt in the air and did a *grand jêté,* one of her favorite ballet steps. Crystal had been taking ballet since she was six, and with her long legs, a big leap like a *grand jêté* could take her halfway across the ballet studio.

Crystal did one last leap up the back steps of the split-level red brick house where she lived with her two older brothers, 15-year-old Arnie and 14-year-old Kyle, and their father.

"Hi!" she called out, as she opened the back door. Then she quickly pulled off her muddy baseball cleats, putting them down neatly in the corner of the laundry room. The little room was filled with sneakers and sporting goods equipment, including two deflated footballs, a bat, and some free weights. Crystal was used to the mess. Because her father was a football coach and her two brothers were totally into sports, there was always sports stuff all over the place. "I'm home!" Crystal continued loudly.

She sniffed the air. A wonderful smell was coming from the kitchen. Arnie or Kyle must have started warming up one of Mrs. Lynch's dinners. Mrs. Lynch came to the Joseph house twice a week to help with the shopping and laundry. While she was there, she would cook a few dinners and then freeze them. Crystal's mother had died when Crystal was five, and no one in her family really had the time or patience for cooking.

"Mmmmm!" Crystal said, heading into the kitchen. "What is it, lasagna?"

"That's right," said her brother Kyle with a smile. "And you're here just in time. We need some salad or something to go with this."

Crystal sighed. Why couldn't her brothers or her father ever do stuff in the kitchen? If she didn't make a salad once in a while, the family probably wouldn't ever get anything green to eat. Just because they did stuff like wash the car and mow the lawn, they acted as if all the cooking and cleaning and stuff was her responsibility as the only girl.

"Thanks, Crys," Kyle said and grinned. "I'm going out for a run. See you soon." Kyle was one of the stars of Bromley High's track and field team, and he trained really hard.

Just then, Crystal heard the front door open. She knew

that it had to be her father and Arnie, back from the weight room at the high school. Mr. Joseph coached the football team there, and Arnie was the star quarterback. In the off-season, Arnie and Mr. Joseph worked out every day to keep in shape. Crystal sometimes wondered if weight-lifting might give her more power with a baseball bat, but she knew better than to ask her father to take her to the weight room with him and Arnie. Her father wasn't overly enthusiastic about her recent interest in baseball. He couldn't understand why she wanted to play ball when she was already such a talented ballerina. But he went to the Pink Parrots' games whenever he could — no matter what he said. And he always cheered loudly.

"Mmm-mmmm," said Mr. Joseph, walking into the kitchen and rubbing his stomach. "It smells great!"

Arnie went over to the refrigerator, pulled out the milk, and took a big swig right out of the carton.

"When's dinner?" he asked Crystal as he wiped the milk off his upper lip with the back of his hand.

Crystal opened the oven and checked the lasagna. "Probably another fifteen minutes," she said. Suddenly she remembered the baseball game and her sixth inning game-saving play.

"Dad," she began, "I have some really exciting news to tell you —"

"Fifteen minutes? Good," her father said, cutting her off. "Enough time for a quick shower." He looked pointedly at Crystal's dirty pink baseball uniform. "And enough time for you to change too, Butterfly. Then you can tell all of us your big news when we're relaxed and sitting around the table." Crystal's father had called her "Butterfly" ever since she was a little girl. It had started because she was so light on her feet that she could run all over the house without anyone even hearing her.

Crystal sighed. Sometimes her father acted like he thought her baseball uniform was some kind of disgrace. Besides, she'd seen her brothers sit down to meals in their sweats or football jerseys. But the more she thought about it, the more she realized how good it would feel to have a hot shower and change. She checked the lasagna one more time and headed toward her room.

Fifteen minutes later, Crystal had showered and changed into a purple sweatshirt and a pair of white jeans that came to just above her ankles. She set the table quickly and served the lasagna onto four plates.

"So, Butterfly," said her father, sitting down and shaking out his napkin, "what's this great news you're all fired up about? Something good happen in school today?"

"No, it was at the game," said Crystal excitedly. "See, we were winning, 9-6, but the bases were loaded with only one out, and this really tough hitter was up for the other team. Anyway, he hit one right toward me. I got him out at first, but the other runners were advancing. Then something just clicked in my head, and I remembered something I read in *Baseball Basics* — you know, one of the books I was telling you about that I got from the library? Anyway, I threw the ball to Julie at second, and we got him in a run-down. I charged him right out of the basepath for the third out, and we won! It was great; I wish you could have seen it. I think Breezy was really psyched, and Ro said she was proud of me for thinking fast. Anyway, I feel like I'm finally beginning to understand how to play."

Crystal paused for a second to catch her breath. She looked excitedly from her father to Arnie to Kyle, waiting for them to congratulate her. After all, this was the first time she had really pulled off a great play in her baseball career. Now her father and brothers would have to pay attention to her baseball news since she was personally responsible for winning the game.

"That's great, Crys," mumbled Kyle through a mouth full of lasagna. "Hey, could you pass the cheese?"

Crystal handed him the jar of parmesan cheese and watched him shake it over his lasagna.

"I remember the first time I got somebody in a pickle," Arnie said with a smile as he took a sip of milk. "It was the same game I hit all three of the home runs we scored."

"I remember that," echoed Kyle. "You were great. Maybe you should have stuck with baseball, too, instead of just football. Who knows? You might have been the next Bo Jackson."

Arnie laughed and took another big bite of lasagna.

"Good going, Butterfly," her father finally said, after swallowing a mouthful of food and clearing his throat. "So tell me, what's happening these days over at Madame Romanov's? Are you going to give a recital there the way you did at your old ballet academy?"

Crystal didn't say anything for a minute. She couldn't believe her family. She had just told them about a major baseball breakthrough for her, and not one of them had shown any excitement whatsoever. All her brothers could do was talk about when they had played baseball and all her father could do was ask about ballet.

Crystal couldn't help it — she was disappointed. Somehow, whenever she wanted to talk about baseball, her father always managed to find a way to change the subject.

"I still remember that beautiful costume you wore in last year's recital," her father went on. "My little girl was the star of the show. What was it you were supposed to be? A poppy, or a daisy?"

"I was the violet in *The Dance of the Flowers*," Crystal explained softly. "And I wasn't the star, Daddy. Diana Lind danced the lead. She was the Flower Queen and I was just one of her subjects."

"Well, as far as I'm concerned, you stole the show, Butterfly," said her father, wiping his mouth with his napkin and standing up from the table. He looked at Arnie and Kyle. "Now, how about you two guys coming out to the garage to help me put some of those boxes up on the storage shelf before you start your homework."

Alone in the kitchen, Crystal cleared the table and stacked the dishes in the dishwasher. She knew her father meant well, but she didn't think it was fair that he and her brothers only seemed to want her to do "girl" things, like ballet dancing and cooking.

Once the dishes were done, Crystal walked down the hall to her room and flopped on her bed, which was a big four-poster canopy bed with pink and white ruffles. It matched her pink shag carpeting perfectly and the pink and white ruffled curtains on the windows. Even her well-stocked bookcase was pink and white.

Crystal opened the drawer of her white wicker night-table and took out her diary. It was really just a yellow spiral notebook, but Crystal wrote in it almost every day. She had started writing in it when she and her father and brothers had moved from Cleveland to Hampstead, Maryland less than two months earlier.

Crystal flipped quickly through the entries at the beginning. They were all a little sad because they were from before she had joined the Pink Parrots and gotten to be friends with everybody on the team. Crystal loved being a Pink Parrot. She loved the challenge of learning all about baseball and applying what she was learning out on the field. It was so different from ballet, where she had to be so perfect and so self-contained all the time. In baseball, one of the most important things was learning how to work together as a team and Crystal enjoyed that a lot. She'd never been on any kind of team before.

Underneath the diary in the drawer was a framed photograph of her mother. Her father had said she could have it, but she kept it in the drawer so her father wouldn't have to see it every time he came into her room. Crystal thought her father must miss her mother very much. He talked about her as if she had been perfect.

Crystal missed her mother too. She remembered helping her bake chocolate chip cookies in their kitchen in Cleveland. And she remembered the way her mother used to sing to her when she tucked her in to bed at night. But that was about all she remembered about her.

She studied the photograph closely. In it, her mother was wearing a blue and white flowered dress and a matching little blue hat. She was smiling softly, and her hands were clasped neatly in her lap.

Crystal let out a long breath and rolled over on her back. She felt that there was no way she could ever be the way her father wanted her to be. She looked up at the big poster of the blue whale over her bed. Crystal loved whales. They were so silent and graceful. Sometimes she thought about what it would be like to be a whale, floating easily through the water, only coming up for a breath of air once in a while.

Crystal took a deep breath, rolled back onto her stomach, opened her yellow notebook, and began to write.

3

"Come on, Crystal," said Jazz, tucking a lock of her honey-blonde hair behind her ear. "Can't you just skip ballet class this one time?"

"Yeah, come on, Crystal," Kim put in. "We're all going to hang out at the Neptune."

Crystal smiled at her friends as they stood in a group on the front steps of Eleanor Roosevelt Junior High. School was over and it was a beautiful sunny day. Crystal was very tempted to take her friends up on their offer, but she really had to go to ballet. She scuffed one of her penny loafers against the ground and then placed her feet in a perfect fourth position. After so many years of taking ballet, she did it without thinking.

"Eddie said he'd make us some of his Dynamite Dip Disasters," wheedled Terry, licking her lips eagerly.

Jazz's parents owned the Neptune diner, and one of their waiters, Eddie Andrews, was famous for his incredible secret ice cream concoctions. All the Parrots thought he was great — and really good-looking.

Crystal shook her head and slung her ballet bag over her shoulder. "No, guys. I'd love to, but I really can't."

"Come on, C.J., what's the big deal if you miss one class?" Breezy asked. "Personally, I can't imagine putting on one of those fluffy pink things and dancing around."

"You mean a tutu, Breeze," Jazz said and giggled.

"Whatever," Breezy commented gruffly. "It's fluffy and pink, isn't it?"

"Not always," Crystal explained with a smile. "Tutus can be any color, depending on the type of performance they're being used for." Either way, Crystal had to admit to herself that she couldn't imagine tough Breezy pirouetting around Madame Romanov's studio in a tutu of any sort, let alone a plain old leotard and tights.

"Anyway, what do you say, C.J.?" Breezy prodded, brushing her dirty-blonde bangs out of her eyes and staring intently at her friend.

"Think of it this way," Crystal explained. "It's kind of like baseball practice. You have to keep going regularly if you want to stay in shape and if you want to be good."

"Yeah, well, I guess that makes sense," Breezy admitted finally. "When you put it that way, at least."

Crystal waved a quick good-bye and walked the two blocks from school to the Hampstead Ballet Academy. As soon as she got there she went straight up the wooden steps, past the reception area to the dressing room. A few other girls were already there, changing into the black leotards and pink tights that were the uniform for every student at Madame Romanov's school. Crystal was in the Sixth Division at the academy, which was the highest.

Crystal, who was graceful by nature, had been taking ballet classes three times a week since she was six. She knew she was good and she really liked ballet, but she didn't think she was great. She also wasn't sure that she had the drive and devotion to ever become great. She used to think she did, but that was before she found out that she loved playing baseball so much.

As Crystal put her bag down on a bench and pulled her baggy gold cable-knit sweater over her head, she heard two cheerful voices call out in unison, "Hi, Crystal, how are you?" It was Amelia and April Gilmore, a pair of red-headed identical twins in the Sixth Division who were always giggling. Crystal liked them because they were so friendly.

Crystal smiled and said hello. The dressing room was beginning to fill up as girls from the Sixth Division arrived and changed clothes. Crystal finished putting on her leotard and tights and hurried into the studio.

Gwen Billings was already there doing *pliés* at the barre and watching herself carefully in the mirror. Crystal had noticed before that Gwen always got to the studio and started warming up ahead of everybody else. Crystal had to admit that no matter what Gwen might be like as a person, she worked really hard in ballet. She was one of the best students in the class. Gwen had started taking ballet with Madame back in the First Division, and she never let anyone forget it. Some of the girls thought she was stuck-up.

Crystal went to the opposite end of the barre and began warming up. She had nothing against Gwen, but she liked to have enough room to extend her long legs when she was stretching. All of the Parrots thought Gwen was almost as big a snob as Lindsay Cunningham, Gwen's best friend. But Crystal looked at her a little differently because she knew her from ballet. She admired Gwen's devotion and the way she worked so hard at ballet, no matter how snobby she might be when she was around Lindsay. Lindsay thought of herself as the queen of their seventh grade class and she happened to hate Breezy and all of the Pink Parrots. Lindsay and Breezy ended up in a lot of arguments because of it. Crystal was convinced that Lindsay just hated the fact that Breezy had gone ahead and formed an all-girls baseball team when everyone said it couldn't be done. Crystal also knew that Lindsay especially hated all of the attention the Pink Parrots got.

Crystal stared at Gwen for a minute, watching how gracefully and perfectly she executed *plié* after *plié*. Gwen was concentrating so hard she obviously had no idea that she had an audience. Crystal thought Gwen was really pretty. She had long curly auburn hair, green eyes, and a cute little upturned nose.

Crystal sighed, turned out her feet in first position,

and watched herself *plié* in the mirror. She frowned critically at her reflection. Her *pliés* weren't quite as graceful as Gwen's. But then, Crystal didn't practice constantly and put ballet above everything else the way Gwen did.

All of a sudden the breathy sounds of April and Amelia giggling brought Crystal back to reality. She noticed that the studio was full and that the rest of the class had arrived and begun warming up at the barre. At that moment Madame Romanov walked in and rapped the floor briskly with her counting stick. Madame, whose graying black hair was pulled into a tight bun at the base of her neck, was dressed in the long black skirt and fringed silk shawl she always wore. She had been teaching at the Academy for years. No one knew exactly how old she was, but she had been a famous ballerina with the Russian Ballet Company when she was young. The hall of the Academy was covered with yellowing photos of her in famous roles: Madame as the Firebird, as Giselle, as the Swan Queen.

Today, as always, Madame carried the long stick that she used to tap out the rhythms of steps on the floor. At the sound of her first few taps, the girls at the barre snapped to attention.

"Hello, my girls. Are we ready?" Madame began brusquely. "Yes? We begin!"

Crystal concentrated as Madame explained the first exercise. Miss Schell, the pianist, began to play.

There were 20 minutes of exercises at the barre and 30 minutes of combinations in the center of the room facing the mirror. Then Madame called to Crystal, Gwen, Allison Robbins, and Leslie Bornstein to change from their soft leather ballet slippers into their pointe shoes. The four of them were the only students in the Sixth Division who were working *en pointe*.

Crystal walked over to the side of the room to change into her pink satin pointe shoes. She noticed that Gwen was sitting right in the middle of the room to lace up her shoes. Gwen seemed so confident about everything. Crystal wished she was that self-assured. She knew some of the other girls in their class interpreted Gwen's confidence as snobbishness, but Crystal honestly admired the way she seemed to always know what she was doing.

Amelia and April stood near Crystal, looking longingly down at her feet.

"Gosh, Crystal," said Amelia, pulling out one of the bobbie pins that had come loose from her red bun and handing it to her sister.

"You're so lucky," echoed April, turning toward Amelia and putting the pin back in its place.

"Neither of us can wait till we get toe shoes," sighed Amelia.

"But Madame says our ankles aren't strong enough yet," sighed April.

"I'm sure you'll both go *en pointe* soon," Crystal reassured them with a smile. "Besides, it's really not as much fun as it looks. Mostly it just hurts your feet a lot."

Crystal was telling the truth about toe dancing. Her feet hurt a lot. She had had her share of blisters since she had started working with her pointe shoes the year before last. But it wasn't exactly true that it was no fun. Now that she was really getting the hang of it, Crystal thought that balancing on the tips of her toes was one of the best things about ballet. The only other thing that had ever made her feel so light and free was rounding the bases after hitting a home run for the Parrots.

Crystal lined up opposite the mirror with Gwen, Allison, and Leslie. The rest of the class was gathering up their things and getting ready to go back to the dressing room when Madame rapped her stick on the floor.

"One moment, girls," she called out. "I want everyone to gather around me, including you four at the barre. I have an important announcement."

Madame proceeded to sit on a tall black stool in front of the class. She didn't need to rap her stick for attention. Everyone was already staring quietly and intently at her.

"The announcement, my girls, is about this year's recital," she continued dramatically.

At Madame's mention of the recital, a murmur of excitement rippled through the class. Crystal noticed Gwen sit up very straight, her eyes glued to Madame. Crystal knew that Gwen had danced the lead in the recital the year before.

"I expect that this year our recital will be extra special," continued Madame, raising her eyebrows and letting her gaze sweep the room. "And now I will tell you why."

The girls waited expectantly while Madame took a deep breath and looked at them.

"This year, we will have the talents of a very special guest to add to our efforts." She turned her head toward the door that led to the reception area. "Nikolai! Nikolai, you may come in now!" she called.

Crystal looked up as a shaggy, blond head peered around the corner of the doorway, and then a guy strode into the room and over to Madame's stool. She heard a little gasp go up from the girls around her. She wondered if they recognized him or something. Maybe he used to be one of Madame's students. Crystal noticed that he had the lean, muscular build and the graceful stride of a dancer. He was dressed in perfectly faded jeans and a navy-blue sweater that picked up the color of his deep blue eyes. He grinned at the girls and tossed a lock of his shaggy blond hair off his forehead. Crystal glanced over at Gwen, who was sitting up so straight and leaning so far forward she looked as if she was about to jump up and run over to the guy.

Madame Romanov reached up and clasped his face in her hands, pulling him toward her and giving him a quick kiss on each cheek, European style.

"This is Nikolai Nabosky," Madame explained, turning to the class and beaming. "He comes to us from

Russia. Nikolai is the prize student of my old friend and student Vasily Lavrosky from Leningrad."

Nikolai smiled at the girls, his blue eyes twinkling.

Crystal nodded to herself. She had read all about Vasily Lavrosky in one of her ballet books; he had been a very famous dancer for the Kirov Ballet in the Soviet Union. Nikolai must be pretty good to be his prize student.

Madame went on. "And now, what good luck for both Nikolai and ourselves — Nikolai has won a scholarship to study ballet in New York, a very great honor at the age of 15. But before he goes there, his teacher Vasily Lavrosky has told him that he must stop here first and visit with his teacher's old friend Madame Romanov."

Nikolai stepped casually forward and smiled again at the class.

"I want to say I am so happy to be in America and meet you, all my new American girlfriends," he said. The class began to giggle. "I love it here in America!" He had a heavy European-sounding accent. He raised both hands to his mouth dramatically and blew a kiss to the crowd of girls in front of him.

A lot of girls in the class sighed audibly. Crystal noticed that Gwen looked as if she was about to fall over. She wondered why.

"And so," Madame continued, "I have spoken with Nikolai, and he has agreed to be the guest star of our recital this year!"

The class murmured excitedly at this news. Even Crystal clasped her hands together at the prospect. She hadn't danced with a boy since the last time she had performed *The Nutcracker* when she was 11. The fact that Nikolai was to be a part of their recital meant that they were going to be doing a more sophisticated ballet than *The Dance of the Flowers*.

"And so, in honor of our guest, this year we will try something exciting," said Madame. "This year, girls, we will be presenting two acts from a very famous ballet, one in which I myself danced both in Paris and New York City — *The Sleeping Beauty*. We will perform Acts Two and Three, and, of course, Nikolai will be our Prince."

Nikolai tossed a lock of blond hair off his forehead and grinned broadly at the crowd of girls.

Everyone in the class began talking enthusiastically. Crystal started feeling more and more enthusiastic too. To have a star pupil from another country — especially one from the Soviet Union, a country famous for its dancers — dance in their recital. Crystal looked around the room at the thrilled faces of the other girls and she started thinking that Nikolai Nabosky might just be the best thing that had ever happened to the Hampstead Ballet Academy.

Madame tapped her stick against the floor for attention one last time. "That's it, that is all for today. My girls *en pointe* should stay, but the rest of you may go."

Just then, Gwen raised her hand and fluttered it daintily in the air to attract Madame's attention.

"Oh, Madame," she called out in her sweetest voice, "you haven't told us about our parts in the recital yet. Who is going to be Sleeping Beauty?" Crystal saw Gwen look over at Nikolai and it appeared as though she even batted her eyelashes at him. This was a little *too* much, Crystal thought.

"Yes, yes," said Madame, "this reminds me. I am calling an extra meeting tomorrow afternoon at four o'clock. At that time, we will talk about all the roles and assign all the parts. Till then, girls."

Crystal, Gwen, Allison, and Leslie stood up and stretched while the other girls left the room. Madame talked to Nikolai for a minute and then after he left, she started putting the four of them through their pointe exercises. Crystal tried to concentrate, but she couldn't help thinking about which part she might get. She was supposed to have baseball practice right after school, but she would just have to leave a little early. Breezy and the others would understand. After all, this was a very special occasion.

After practice Crystal changed quickly back into her sweater and jeans. On her way out the door, Crystal heard the sound of music playing. She wondered who could be dancing so late, so she stopped by the studio and peered inside. Nikolai had changed into a white T-shirt and a pair of black warm-ups. Under Madame's direction, he was practicing a series of steps.

Crystal stood and stared as Nikolai kicked up his long muscular legs and went into a *tour-jêté*, turning his entire body around in mid-air. Crystal had never seen anyone jump that high. He landed as softly as a cat and went into a series of pirouettes. Crystal, who was one of the few girls in the Sixth Division who could do a triple pirouette, was amazed to count six turns in Nikolai's set. He finished with a *grand jêté,* leaping so high in the air that he looked like he was about to hit the ceiling.

As Crystal walked home, she searched her mind, trying to remember everything she could about the ballet, *The Sleeping Beauty*, especially about Acts Two and Three. She knew there was a princess who was put under a spell, who couldn't wake up until she was kissed by the Prince. Crystal was pretty sure this happened at the end of the ballet, probably in Act Three. She would have to look up the details in the big *Encyclopedia of the Great Ballets* that her father had given her for Christmas the year before.

4

Crystal sat in bed with the *Encyclopedia of the Great Ballets* open across her lap. She found *The Sleeping Beauty* in the table of contents and flipped to the page.

Looking quickly over the Prologue and Act One, Crystal learned that there was once a princess born in a kingdom. The king and queen gave a large party in honor of their baby, and the princess's many fairy godmothers attended, bringing gifts. The one fairy who was not invited, the Evil Fairy, was so angry that she put a spell on the baby, saying that the princess would die one day from pricking her finger. The good Lilac Fairy, the leader of all the fairies, tried to lighten the curse, promising that the princess would not die from the finger prick, but would fall into a deep sleep for 100 years. The rest of the kingdom would sleep also, until a handsome prince kissed the princess and woke her from her sleep. Hearing this, the king gave an order that all needles be kept away from the princess for the rest of her life.

In the next scene, at the princess's 16th birthday party,

the Evil Fairy arrived disguised as a guest and gave the princess a birthday gift. The present turned out to be a sewing spindle, and the princess was pricked by its needle and fell into a deep sleep.

Crystal settled down to concentrate on Acts Two and Three, the part of the ballet that would be performed at the recital. She read:

As Act 2 opens, the entire kingdom has been asleep for 100 years. Fairies dance in the woods, where a prince from another kingdom is hunting. He is alone, and as night falls, the spirit of the sleeping princess appears to him. The prince and the princess dance together and fall in love. Finally, the spirit of the princess drifts away, and the prince vows to find the Sleeping Beauty and wake her. The good Lilac Fairy appears and tells him to sail across the lake to the palace of the king, where the princess lies asleep.

In Act 3, the prince sails to the kingdom and finds the princess asleep. He kisses her, she wakes up, and they dance together. As the Lilac Fairy promised, the rest of the kingdom also awakens. There is a great wedding celebration, and the prince and princess dance together again.

Crystal closed the book and took a deep breath. To dance the part of the princess with a real live Russian ballet dancer as the prince would be a dream come true. Then again, Nikolai was probably such a great dancer that she might look really bad in comparison. And he would know everything she did wrong.

Besides, Crystal had only been at the school for less

than two months. There was no way Madame Romanov would choose her to play such an important role after working with her for such a short time. There were girls in the Sixth Division that Madame had worked with for a very long time — like Gwen.

And after all, Crystal decided, there were a lot of other good parts in the ballet. The fairies, for example — they had such beautiful names: the Fairy of the Crystal Fountain, the Fairy of the Songbirds, the Fairy of the Golden Vine, the Fairy of the Enchanted Garden, and, of course, the Lilac Fairy. Crystal knew she would be happy dancing any part. The Princess would probably be too much pressure anyway, she figured.

Crystal must have dozed off thinking about the ballet. When she woke up the next morning, the ballet encyclopedia was still next to her in the bed. She had a dim memory of dreaming something about fairies and enchanted kingdoms, and she thought she remembered seeing Nikolai's face, but she couldn't be sure.

Later that day, at lunch period, Crystal carried her tray over to the table where Breezy, Jazz, and Kim were already sitting.

"Hey, C.J.!" Breezy called out to her. "How's it going?"

"Hi, Crystal," said Kim cheerfully.

Jazz moved over on the bench to make room.

"Hi, guys," Crystal replied, putting her tray on the table and sitting down on the bench next to Jazz.

"How'd you do on that social studies quiz, Crystal?" Kim asked, biting into an apple. "That was a total killer. I hate pop quizzes."

"Really," Breezy agreed. "What's the purpose of surprising us?"

"I know what you mean," Crystal replied. In a weird sort of way, Crystal wished she had been surprised like the rest of her friends. But Mr. Carrea, the social studies teacher, was pretty easy to read. Since she had moved to Hampstead, Crystal had kept track of all of his pop quizzes. Every 13th school day, he had another one. So Crystal put extra time into studying on the night of the 12th school day. And so far, it had paid off.

Crystal had never told her friends about Mr. Carrea's system because she was worried that he might switch to every 10th school day, or every 15th school day. Crystal would hate it if her friends all studied really hard one night, only to find that there was no quiz the next day. She would have to study his system a little longer to be certain. Then she would tell her friends about it. Crystal didn't like to talk about anything unless she had thought it through and understood it perfectly.

"What else is new?" Breezy asked, slurping her milk.

"Nothing," Crystal replied, wishing she had watched the Orioles game the night before. Breezy loved to rehash games. But then she remembered about the ballet and Nikolai.

"Actually, I do have something to tell you guys

about," she began excitedly. "There's this boy —"

"Oh, yeah," Breezy interrupted, "I know what you're going to say, C.J. I heard all about him. He's out of hand, isn't he?"

Crystal looked up, startled. Breezy had heard all about Nikolai? How could that be? Crystal hadn't even told them about the ballet or anything yet.

"You have?" she asked, amazed. "But how do *you* know about him, Breezy?"

Breezy gave Crystal a strange look. "What do you mean, how do *I* know about him? Everyone knows about him. It's all over Emblem."

"It is?" asked Crystal. "Why does everyone know about Nikolai?"

"Nikolai?" Breezy asked, sounding totally confused. "Who are you talking about, C.J.? There's no one named Nikolai on the Dudley's Bar and Grill team."

"Dudley's Bar and Grill?"

"Right," said Breezy, opening a bag of potato chips. "James Hsu. You know, that guy that seemed to come out of nowhere. He hit three home runs last week — in one game! Who are you talking about? Did this guy hit three homers, too? That's wild. And Emblem used to be a pitcher's league. It's definitely the place for a hitter to be now."

Crystal started laughing. Baseball really was all Breezy thought about.

"Come on," Breezy continued, "who's this Nichols

guy? What position does he play?"

Crystal laughed even harder at the idea of Nikolai Nabosky in a baseball uniform. She was pretty sure they didn't even play baseball in the Soviet Union. And even if they did, Nikolai didn't seem the type to play.

"What's so funny, Crystal?" Kim asked, curious. "I didn't think three homers was all that funny."

"Nothing," Crystal finally said, when she caught her breath. "It's just that Breezy and I were talking about two totally different people. You see, my dance academy is doing a real ballet this year for our recital. Nikolai is a dancer who's going to be in the performance."

"I didn't think any guys in Hampstead took ballet," Breezy said. "Does he play baseball too? Oh, well, it's probably too late for him to join a team anyway."

"Nikolai isn't from Hampstead," Crystal explained. "He's from Russia. You know, the Soviet Union. He just stopped here on his way to New York. He's going to study ballet there. I really don't think he plays baseball anyway."

"Wow," Jazz said, her face lighting up. Crystal was glad someone else seemed impressed about her news. She really wished that Breezy would take other things as seriously as she took baseball. Ballet was hard work, too, after all.

"Is he cute?" Jazz continued. Crystal sighed. She should have known that Jazz wouldn't be impressed by the ballet. It was the boy who had gotten her attention.

"I don't know," Crystal admitted. She hadn't really thought about it. He did look as if he would be a great dancer though. He had that dancer's walk.

"Well, what does he look like?" Jazz persisted.

Crystal shot a look at Breezy, but she was deep in a conversation with Kim about the Orioles' game the night before. It was obvious that Breezy wasn't really interested in Crystal's news since it wasn't about a baseball player.

"Um," Crystal began, and then paused. She closed her eyes, trying to picture Nikolai. She wanted to give Jazz an accurate description. "He's taller than I am by about four inches. But that's probably because he's fifteen."

"He's fifteen?!" Jazz exclaimed, sounding excited.

"Yes," Crystal replied, continuing with her description. "And he's got longish, kind of shaggy blond hair and deep blue eyes."

"Wow," Jazz said breathlessly. "Maybe I should start taking ballet."

Just then, Crystal noticed Lindsay Cunningham walk into the lunchroom with Beth Douglas, Gwen Billings, and Molly Cooper. They paused for a moment, as if they wanted to make sure that everyone had noticed their entrance. Lindsay slowly flipped her long, white-blonde hair off her shoulder.

"I can't even believe I used to be friends with those guys," Jazz whispered, rolling her eyes at Crystal. "They're such phonies."

"There's a table over there, Lindsay," Beth pointed out loudly.

Crystal had noticed that Lindsay and her friends were definitely the loudest group of girls at Eleanor Roosevelt Junior High. Even though Crystal knew that they were only loud because they wanted to attract everyone's attention, it didn't make it any easier for Crystal to stomach it.

"We can't sit there," Lindsay contradicted Beth. "We *always* sit at the same table. People should know better than to sit at our table." Lindsay flipped her hair again and glared at Breezy.

Crystal suddenly realized that the Pink Parrots were sitting at Lindsay's table. She glanced at Breezy, who was calmly eating her lunch. Lindsay was right — she and her friends always sat at the same table. And Crystal was sure that Breezy knew that, just as everyone else did. But Breezy never paid attention to stuff like that. She didn't care about "Lindsay's table" or "the jocks' table." If there was an empty seat in the cafeteria, Breezy sat in it. Crystal admired the fact that Breezy always did her own thing no matter who got mad about it.

When it became obvious to Lindsay that none of the girls was going to move from "her" table, she sighed and headed for the only empty table in the cafeteria — right behind the Pink Parrots.

Lindsay and her friends put their trays down loudly and they all sat down.

"Now remember, Gwen," Lindsay said so everyone within a four-table radius could hear them, "you promised to save me a front row seat at this recital. I want to get a look at this guy close up."

Crystal was sure they were talking about the Hampstead Ballet Academy recital.

"Really," said Beth, "especially if he's as cute as you say. He has an accent, right?"

"Beth, please," Lindsay replied. "He's from another country. Of course he has an accent."

"Oh, yeah," Beth answered.

"Linz, I'm sure that'll be no problem at all," Gwen said, answering Lindsay's question. "I can probably reserve the whole front row."

Crystal wondered if Gwen knew somebody in the ticket office or something. It was really hard to get seats in the front row. Crystal didn't think she had ever sat in the front row at a recital — much less been able to reserve the whole row.

"Oh, good," said Breezy, who obviously had not been listening to the conversation at Lindsay and Gwen's table. "Here comes Terry. I want to talk about our signals. We have to make sure we get those new ones straight before the big game against Dudley's."

Terry walked over and plopped down next to Breezy. Crystal tried to follow their conversation about pitching signals because she wanted to know everything about baseball. But she couldn't help turning an ear toward what Gwen and Lindsay were saying behind her. Maybe Gwen knew something about *The Sleeping Beauty* that she didn't.

"Oh, I just know it's going to be the biggest thing the Ballet Academy has ever done," Gwen said loudly.

"So, what's the show you're doing again?" Molly asked. "*Sleeping Beauty*? I thought that was a movie or something."

"You didn't tell us you were doing *Sleeping Beauty*," Jazz suddenly said, turning to Crystal, her blue eyes shining. "That's *so* romantic. It was my favorite story when I was little."

Crystal nodded and went on listening.

"Well, I'm not really sure of all the details," Gwen replied. "But I know it's a very famous and classic ballet. I'm sure the story must be a lot like the movie."

"Oh, my gosh, Gwen!" Lindsay suddenly exclaimed. "You didn't tell us you were dancing a *romance* with a gorgeous guy from Russia. What if he becomes famous? Imagine, you can say you danced a lead role with Nikolai! Do you get to kiss him?"

Crystal froze in surprise. What did Lindsay mean, saying that Gwen was going to *star* in *The Sleeping Beauty*? Madame hadn't cast anyone in the role yet. It sounded as if Gwen was pretty positive about it, though. Maybe she knew something that Crystal didn't. Gwen *was* really good. She probably always got the lead. And Gwen had studied with Madame Romanov for years.

Why would Madame choose anyone else?

"Just think," sighed Gwen. "A role made famous by the best ballerinas in the world — the Princess in *The Sleeping Beauty*. And now I get to dance it with one of Russia's most promising young dancers."

"Crystal, you didn't tell us that Gwen was starring in this recital with that Nikolai guy," Jazz said quietly, cutting into Crystal's thoughts.

Gwen went on before Crystal had a chance to answer, "Of course, Madame hasn't *officially* announced that I'm the Princess yet, but I just know I am. After all, who else could she pick?"

Jazz spooned up the last of her yogurt and looked at Crystal expectantly.

"So," Terry said loudly to Breezy, "like we said, three fingers is the sidearm fastball."

"I really didn't know that, Jazz," Crystal said, not paying attention to Terry and Breezy.

Breezy, Terry, and Kim all stopped talking and looked at Crystal in surprise.

"What are you talking about, C.J.?" asked Breezy. "When Terry shows three fingers it always means the sidearm fastball. Do you think there's a problem with that? Maybe we should change it. Did you read something about signals?"

"I'm not talking about *that*," said Crystal. "I was talking about that ballet recital. Gwen just said she's going to be the lead in *Sleeping Beauty*."

"They chose parts already?" Kim asked. "What part are you?"

"I don't know," Crystal admitted, still a little confused. She wondered what part she would get and hoped it would be one of the fairies.

"Well, how does Gwen know what part she got?" Terry asked.

"I don't know that either," Crystal repeated. "I guess I'll find out later on today at ballet."

"You've got ballet today?" Breezy asked her in astonishment. "You mean, you're not going to practice? We've got that big game coming up against Dudley's. You can't just cut out of practice, you know."

Crystal sighed. "Don't worry, Breezy. I'll be at practice. Ballet is later."

"Well, then," Breezy began, as if everything was settled. "I'm sure you'll get a part in this recital thing. Now, we've got to concentrate on this game. If we want to stay in good position going into the All-Star Game, we've got to win at least five games." Crystal nodded and tried to listen as Breezy went over the strengths and weaknesses of Dudley's Bar and Grill. But she couldn't help thinking about *The Sleeping Beauty*.

It was really hard doing both ballet and baseball sometimes. Crystal felt kind of torn between the two of them. She knew that Gwen was totally dedicated to ballet. Gwen was always warming up before anyone else got to the studio. She stayed late a lot and she even took more ballet lessons than Crystal.

But Crystal didn't know if she could spend that much time on ballet; baseball and her friends meant too much to her. But she also loved to dance. Why couldn't she just keep doing both, Crystal wondered.

5

"All right, you birds!" Ro yelled at the Parrots that afternoon at practice. "We've got a tough game coming up and we've got to be ready for it!"

Crystal watched Ro pace up and down in front of the dugout bench. The coach's ponytail was hairsprayed straight up on top of her head like a whale's spout. Ro was nothing like Crystal had expected an Emblem coach to be. But then again, the Pink Parrots were not an ordinary team, so they deserved an extraordinary coach.

Blowing a major bubble with her gum, Ro continued. "Now, I think we've got to work on a few things today that might make the difference between winning and losing against Dudley's: bunting and sliding. Even though it's not for three weeks, we've got to be prepared because they're tough. We've got some pretty solid hitting and defense out there."

Slides were first. Ro had everyone gather around home plate.

"Now, Breezy's going to demonstrate a few variations

of slides," Ro said, nodding to Breezy, who was standing by third. "And then everyone's going to try each kind and work on it until it's perfect. Okay?"

Perfect? Crystal hoped it wouldn't take too long. She had ballet at 4:00 and she couldn't be late.

"And remember, birds," Ro continued. "You should never slide unless you have to. If the baseman is waiting for the ball to make the tag, you've got to slide. But that's basically it. We don't want anyone taking any risks here. Any questions?"

"What about using a slide to break up a double play?" Crystal asked, remembering something she had read a few weeks ago in a chapter on sliding.

"Oh, right," Ro replied, hitting her forehead with her hand. "How could I forget that? You should also slide if you're running into a double play situation. Even if you get tagged, you might be able to knock the baseman off balance or knock the ball out of his hand or glove. That way, he can't make the throw to another base."

"Okay, Breeze!" Ro called out. "Let's see a hook slide first, all right, hon?"

Breezy nodded and ran toward home.

"Now, the hook slide can be made to either side of the base or plate, depending upon where the baseman is standing," Ro explained as Breezy sprinted toward home. "You should be on your side, and your top leg should hook, or bend, while the other leg remains straight. If you're sliding into the right side of the bag, your top leg will be the left leg, and if you're sliding into the left side of the bag, it will be your right leg that bends." Breezy suddenly dropped on her bottom and slid into the left side of the plate. Her right leg was bent and her left leg and foot slid past the bag. Her right toe caught the bag and her body was almost completely flat on the ground. "Notice how flat she is on the ground. This way she can try to slide *under* the baseman's tag."

Breezy stood up and dusted herself off. "You can also slide in with both feet pointed at the bag and then as you slide past the bag, bend either leg and hook the bag with that toe," she added.

"Right," Ro agreed. "And remember, timing is everything. You want to stop just as you tag the bag. It would be bad to hit the bag and keep going, you know what I mean?"

Crystal laughed with everyone else. She could just see sliding into second and not stopping until she was in leftfield or something.

"Good, Breeze," Ro complimented her captain. "Let's see a hand tag this time."

Breezy trotted back to third base as Ro continued. "This slide is basically the same as the variation of the hook slide."

"Okay, hon!" Ro called out loudly. Breezy started sprinting toward home plate. "As she slides past, watch how Breezy tags the plate with her left hand." Again Breezy dropped on her backside and slid in. This time, both feet pointed right behind the plate.

Breezy stopped as if on a dime just as her hand touched the base. "And stay as low or flat as possible," Ro finished as Breezy jumped up and trotted back to third without waiting for more instructions.

"Do the bent leg or straight-in slide, Breezy!" Ro yelled out.

Breezy gave a thumbs-up signal and ran toward home plate.

"This slide isn't as good to use as the hook slide," Ro continued. "It's easier to hurt yourself. You should use this slide only when you might need to stand up really quickly. You know, if you think the baseman might miss the ball and you can run on to the next base."

"Here I come!" Breezy yelled as she ran in. She dropped into her slide with her left leg bent under her and the right stretched out straight. Her front foot hit the plate, but Breezy kept going, her batting helmet falling off in the process. In a flash, Breezy just popped up and looked ready to take off again.

"See how Breezy used the plate and her front foot to get back up," Ro pointed out. "This is a dangerous slide, though. So only use it when you have to."

"Can I do the headfirst one now?" Breezy asked, putting back on her batting helmet. "That's my favorite."

"Okay, okay," Ro agreed with a sigh. "Now, girls, this is a really dangerous slide. You slide in headfirst toward the bag, so you might get hit in the head with the bag, the ball, or even the baseman's feet. So be careful."

"Yeah, but it's a lot of fun!" Breezy exclaimed. "The headfirst slide is Rickey Henderson's favorite slide."

"Rickey who?" Jazz asked, sounding totally confused.

Breezy groaned. "I can't believe my own cousin doesn't know who Rickey Henderson is," she said, shaking her head. "It's unbelievable. There's no way we can be related."

"He plays for the Oakland A's," Crystal explained.

"Don't worry about it, Jazz," Kim cut in. "It's not important. Let's just watch Breezy do this slide."

"All right," Ro said. "Because this slide is risky, you should only use it when you're sliding one or two feet, at the most. Basically, you use it to dive back to a base. Like when you forget to tag up and it's a fly ball that might be caught. Okay? Breezy, just dive back into home plate. Pretend it's another base, since there's no reason to dive back to home."

Breezy walked out about three feet from the plate. She pretended that she was watching the action on the field and then suddenly dove headfirst into the plate, touching it with her hand.

"Any questions?" Ro asked, and then paused for a moment. "Okay, Parrots, line up by third and come down one at a time doing the hook slide."

Half an hour later, Crystal was completely covered with dirt, but she had the hook slide down pat. She didn't think she'd ever use the headfirst slide. In fact, she and

Jazz were the only ones on the team who couldn't do it in practice—actually, Jazz wouldn't do it at all. But Crystal had tried. There was something about the slide that made Crystal feel kind of . . . vulnerable. She wished she could be like Breezy and just fling herself onto the ground without worrying about it.

"Birds!" Ro called, while everyone was busy brushing off their sweats. "Time to bunt. Crystal, you've got a picture-perfect bunt. You can be my demonstrator."

Crystal picked up a bat and stepped into the batter's box. "Breezy, I need you to lob the ball in to Crystal," Ro continued. "Birds, remember that you want the ball to drop dead — like it's been shot — when you bunt. The less the ball travels in a bunt, the better it is. And you can aim it. If there's a runner on third that you want to score, bunt the ball toward first base. That way, while the first baseman is concerned with getting you out, the runner on third will score. All right Breezy, lob it in. Terry, would you catch?"

Terry strapped on her catcher's equipment. Ro always made Terry put on all of her pads and her mask no matter what. Crystal thought that Terry would probably do it anyway because she took catching very seriously. Breezy threw the ball in lightly. Crystal waited until it was right in front of her and then quickly turned toward Breezy. She let the bat slide through her right hand until her top hand was behind the label. Then she pushed her bat toward the ball, ever so slightly. The ball bounced off the bat and fell to the ground three feet in front of home plate.

"Great bunt!" Ro exclaimed. "Of course, you girls realize that the bunt didn't go very far because the pitch wasn't that fast. Now, the trick to bunting is to *push* at the ball, not swing at it. Who wants to try next? Julie?"

By the time they had all finished practicing, Crystal still had 15 minutes to get to ballet. She breathed a sigh of relief. It was nice how things worked out sometimes.

"Before you all go, birds," Ro said, "we're going to do a relaxation/visualization exercise."

"A what?" Breezy asked.

Crystal knew that Breezy sometimes questioned Ro's training methods — they were a little bizarre. But they all had to admit that in the end, weird or not, Ro's techniques really did seem to work.

Ro laughed. "Let's get in a big circle out in centerfield," she instructed.

When everyone was in place, Ro stepped into the center of the circle. "Now take two steps back," she continued.

"Giant steps?" Jazz asked.

"Regular steps," Ro replied, as everyone moved back a little. "All right, that's good. Now lie down with your feet pointing in."

"This is definitely weird," Breezy whispered to Crystal. "I feel like a spoke in a bicycle wheel."

"Good comparison, Breezy," Ro cut in suddenly,

laughing. "The Pink Parrots as a team are like the wheel and each of you is a spoke. Without all of its spokes, the wheel doesn't turn right. Each spoke is needed for the wheel to do its job."

"We're going to roll around?" Jazz asked, sounding confused.

"We're not really wheels, Jazz," Breezy said, rolling her eyes at Crystal. "It's just a comparison, you know?"

"Oh, okay," Jazz replied, sounding unconvinced.

"Our job is to play well together and win," Ro said. "Now I want everyone to close their eyes and think about playing Dudley's. Can you see it?"

"See what?" Jazz asked. "All I see is black."

"Jazz!" Breezy yelled, sitting up.

"Just concentrate, hon," Ro said. "Think about playing baseball, okay?"

"All right, but I still don't see anything," Jazz replied.

Breezy lay down again, grumbling.

"Okay, Parrots," Ro continued in a soft voice. "Now, it's time for the game against Dudley's. We're there and we're all warming up, okay?"

"If you say so, Ro," Jazz piped up.

"Shut up, Jazz!" Breezy hissed.

"Girls, this is a team," Ro reprimanded gently. "The purpose of this exercise is to internalize our view of ourselves as a team. Each of us has to learn to count on the person lying next to her. This circle is unbroken."

Crystal looked at her watch nervously. She had to

leave in the next few minutes or she would be late for ballet. This didn't seem like the best time to jump up and run off though — the circle would be broken. But she really didn't think she had a choice.

"Uh, Ro," Crystal interrupted a little hesitantly. "I have to go now. I'm going to be late for ballet."

"We'll only be here another fifteen minutes or so," Ro replied. "Can you wait until then?"

"I'm sorry," Crystal apologized. "I really can't. I have to go." She stood up and started walking toward the bleachers, where she'd left her stuff.

"Wait a minute!" Breezy called after her. "You can't just take off like that. This visualization stuff could be important. We need you here."

"Really," Jazz added. "You're a spoke! Our bicycle wheel won't turn without you."

"Sorry, guys," Crystal called back. "I don't have a choice."

Breezy stood up. "I can't believe you're running out on the team!" she yelled. "It sounds to me as if you *do* have a choice — and you've definitely made it!"

Crystal paused and started to walk back. Then she stopped. Madame would be really mad if she was any later than she already was for ballet. She had to run if she was going to make it in time. "Breezy . . ." she began.

"Fine, C.J.!" Breezy said loudly, lying back down again. "Go off to your little dance class. See if I care. We'll just make do with one less spoke. No big deal."

Crystal felt tears welling up in the corners of her eyes. Why couldn't Breezy understand that Madame, everyone at the ballet academy, and her family were all counting on her to be in this recital? She couldn't let them down. Meanwhile, she was really late. She spun around and headed for the bleachers in a rush.

6

Crystal ran toward the Ballet Academy as fast as her long legs could carry her. She was the fastest runner on the Parrots. But she knew she didn't have much of a chance of running the 11 blocks to Madame's in less than five minutes.

Breathing hard, Crystal burst into the reception area and rushed to the dressing room. She was still so hot and sweaty from practice that she practically had to peel off her baseball uniform. She brushed the tears out of her eyes. She couldn't think about the Pink Parrots now. As fast as she could, she pulled on her regulation leotard and tights. Still stuffing her feet into her ballet slippers, she hurried down the hall to the studio.

The rest of the Sixth Division was already there and changed, and sitting in a group on the floor in front of Madame. As Crystal slipped in between the twins and Leslie, she noticed Nikolai off to one side, chewing on a toothpick. He was staring right at her with this strange expression on his face. It made Crystal uncomfortable, and she felt her cheeks beginning to get warm. But then she suddenly realized that not only Nikolai but everyone else in the room — including Madame — was looking at her too. What was it? Was she *that* late for class?

"Miss Joseph," Madame addressed her in the formal tone she only adopted when she was very serious about something. "I believe your, uh, makeup, does not fall within Academy dress regulations."

What was Madame talking about, Crystal wondered. She wasn't wearing any makeup as far as she knew.

"Your cheeks, Crystal," Amelia whispered, nudging her in the ribs.

"You've got big black smudges under your eyes," April echoed softly.

Crystal's hand crept up to her face. To her horror, she felt the eye-black smudged there. With all her rushing to get into the studio, she had forgotten to take it off. How embarrassing! Blushing deeply, she quickly grabbed the tissue April offered and frantically rubbed it off. All the Parrots had been wearing eye-black for practice because of the glare. Crystal tried not to look at anyone in the room, but she could hear the unmistakable sound of giggling.

"All right, all right," said Madame, tapping her stick. "That is quite enough. Now that we are all here, we can begin. I will start by announcing who will dance the major roles in our production of *The Sleeping Beauty.*"

Madame proceeded to take out a list from the pocket

of her long black skirt and slip on her gold-framed half-moon reading glasses. Then she cleared her throat.

"As you all know, Nikolai Nabosky has agreed to dance the part of the Prince."

At the mention of his name, Nikolai grinned and raised his hand to his forehead in a mock salute.

"The part of the Fairy of the Crystal Fountain will be danced by Leslie Bornstein," Madame continued.

Leslie, who was sitting next to Crystal, gasped.

Madame continued reading. "The Fairy of the Golden Vine will be Allison Robbins. The Fairy of the Songbirds will be danced by Amelia Gilmore, and the Fairy of the Enchanted Garden will be April Gilmore." Amelia and April gave each other a quick little hug. "And, then of course, we have the Lilac Fairy, the leader of all the Fairies."

Crystal held her breath. She knew that the Lilac Fairy was a big role, probably the biggest next to the Princess. It was the Lilac Fairy who was responsible for reducing the curse put on the Princess by the Evil Fairy, and she also led the Prince to the sleeping Princess.

"The Lilac Fairy," Madame announced, "will be danced by Gwen Billings, and the part of the Princess will be danced by Crystal Joseph."

Crystal's mouth dropped open in surprise, and her whole body felt numb with shock. That couldn't be right. Gwen was supposed to be the Princess. She had just announced it at lunch. How was it possible that Crystal was the Princess? Madame must have made a mistake. But the next thing Crystal knew, Amelia and April were hugging her and Leslie was patting her on the back.

"Congratulations, Crystal!" Leslie exclaimed.

"You really deserve it," said Amelia with a smile.

"You'll be great," added April.

Crystal couldn't believe it. Then she *had* heard Madame correctly. *She* was actually going to dance the lead in the recital with Nikolai!

Crystal was aware that Madame was still reading names off the list, assigning the smaller parts, but she wasn't listening. Instead, her mind was racing. She wondered what it would be like to practice with Nikolai. She hoped she'd be able to keep up with him. He was obviously such a professional. It made Crystal totally nervous just thinking about dancing with an almost-famous Russian ballet dancer. And he was probably used to dancing with other almost-famous ballerinas. What would he think of her not-almost-famous self compared to them?

Madame paused for a minute after she had finished reading the list. "Finally, I want all of the girls *en pointe* to learn the parts of the Lilac Fairy and the Princess in addition to their own parts so that we have understudies for those roles. And now, ladies, I will begin the first rehearsal today by working with the five Fairies," Madame concluded. "The rest of you are free to go."

Crystal stood up with the rest of the girls. She couldn't

help noticing that Gwen was still sitting on the floor, her lips pursed tightly together and her cheeks flushed. Gwen's conversation in the lunchroom had made it very clear that she had expected to be the Princess.

As Crystal walked toward the door of the studio, Madame motioned for her to come over to the stool where she was sitting.

"Miss Joseph, I will need much extra rehearsal time with you and the Prince if we are to get this recital ready in time. Please come back the day after tomorrow, and I will work with the two of you together."

"Yes, Madame," Crystal replied, her heart still racing.

As Crystal headed for the dressing room, she felt a tap on her shoulder. She turned around and found herself looking right into Nikolai's deep blue eyes. That was a rare occurrence for Crystal, who was taller than almost all of the boys in her class.

"Congratulations!" he said, holding out his hand and breaking into one of his grins. "I think you will make a most wonderful princess."

Crystal shook Nikolai's hand quickly, surprised that she was so pleased by his compliment.

"Um, no, I mean y-yes," she stammered, smiling shyly back at him. "Thank you."

"You are most very welcome," said Nikolai, bowing from the waist.

When Crystal got to the dressing room, her heart was beating with excitement. All the other girls had already changed and gone home, so she just stood there for a minute marveling over what had happened. She, Crystal Joseph, had been chosen to dance the lead in one of the most famous ballets ever performed. It was better than anything she had ever dreamed.

"Congratulations," someone suddenly said. Crystal turned quickly and saw Gwen standing there with her hands planted firmly on her hips and a very serious expression on her face.

"Umm . . . thanks," Crystal replied with a smile. She knew that Gwen must be very disappointed, and she was impressed that she had come over to congratulate her anyway. "Congratulations to you too. The Lilac Fairy is a great —"

"Look, Crystal," Gwen cut her off before she could finish. "We all know that it wasn't a question of talent. You only got the part because you're so tall."

Before Crystal could even reply, Gwen turned on her heel and left the dressing room. Crystal sank down onto the changing bench in the middle of the room and sighed. Poor Gwen must be really upset to say something like that. It couldn't be true, could it? Well, either way, Crystal was just going to have to try her hardest to dance the part of the Princess perfectly. Her stomach flip-flopped at the prospect. Between Nikolai's expectations and Gwen's disappointment, Crystal started feeling more and more nervous. She didn't think she'd ever been so nervous about anything in her entire life.

7

Crystal felt as if she was floating all the way home. She couldn't remember ever being so excited about anything. She noticed her dad's yellow station wagon parked in the driveway and bounded up the back steps. She knew he'd be pleased at her news, and Crystal loved making her father happy.

Crystal banged open the back door and flew into the kitchen without taking off her shoes or putting down her baseball stuff. She skidded to a stop in front of the kitchen table and paused to catch her breath. Her father and her brothers stared at her.

"What's up, Butterfly?" Mr. Joseph asked. "You look as if you're about to burst."

"Yeah, Crys," Kyle commented, leaning against the refrigerator and taking a swig of milk.

"Out with it, sis," Arnie said, folding his arms across his chest and smiling at Crystal.

"Well, my ballet class is doing a performance of *The Sleeping Beauty* and this famous Russian dancer, who's a friend of Madame Romanov's, is dancing the part of the Prince," Crystal blurted out. "And guess who is dancing the part of the Princess?"

"Congratulations, Butterfly!" Mr. Joseph exclaimed, walking over to his daughter and giving her a big hug. "I always knew you were the star of the show!"

"Hey, that's great!" echoed Kyle, raising his milk glass to toast his sister.

"Another Joseph hits the road to fame and fortune," commented Arnie, grinning broadly at Crystal.

"I can't believe it," Crystal murmured softly. "I can't believe Madame actually chose me to be the Princess."

"Well, I can, Butterfly," Crystal's father said loudly. "In fact, I think we should all go out to Anthony's for some Italian food to celebrate."

"Really?" breathed Crystal.

"Yes, really," said her father. "After all, it's not every day my daughter gets picked to be the star. I'd say that's a very special occasion."

"Thanks, Dad," Crystal said, giving her father another hug. Crystal loved going to Anthony's. The Josephs hadn't been out to dinner in a while, and they almost never went anywhere during the week. She smiled as she walked down the hallway to her room, thinking about how happy she felt this evening and how wonderful her family was — especially her dad.

The next day after school, Crystal stood in front of her locker pulling out her books and thinking about how to apologize to Breezy for running out on practice the day before. All the other Parrots had congratulated her about getting the part of the Princess — except for Breezy. Crystal understood how Breezy felt; the team was so important to her. Crystal also knew it was up to her to make the first move because admitting she was sorry was something Breezy never did — even if she was.

Crystal took a deep breath and slammed her locker door shut with a bang. It was now or never, and Breezy's friendship and playing baseball were too important to her not to do something about it right away. She knew Breezy had had to go see Mr. Johnson, the science teacher, after class, so she had a few more minutes to figure out what to say.

Just then she heard the unmistakable sound of Breezy's laughter coming from down the hall. Crystal grabbed her bag and headed in that direction. Breezy was standing in front of her locker, laughing at something Peter Tolhurst had said. Crystal hesitated for a minute, but then forced herself to walk over to them.

"Hi, guys," Crystal said with a small smile.

"Hey," Peter replied, smiling back. "So, Breeze, like I said, you've got to watch out for Jimmy Hsu. He came out of nowhere. Got to run. See you guys later." With that he was gone, leaving the two girls alone.

"Umm, Breezy, I . . . ummm . . . I wanted to apologize for walking out on the team like that yesterday," Crystal stuttered, her gaze focused on her feet.

"Look, C.J.," Breezy cut in before Crystal could say anything else. "It's okay. But, I mean, it's really important that we stick together as a team if we want to win our games, and we can't do that if everyone's not there. Hey, how'd your ballet thing go? I hear you did great," Breezy concluded, slapping her friend on the back and grinning broadly at Crystal.

"There's the star!" Terry exclaimed loudly as she came up next to Breezy and Crystal. "So, where are we going to celebrate?"

"Yeah," Breezy agreed immediately. "Now that you're the star in that dance thing, we have to celebrate."

"That's okay," Crystal replied shyly. "I mean, we don't have to do anything special just because of that. It's not that big a deal."

"Come on, C.J.," Breezy said. "It's important to you, right? So if it's important to you, then it's important to us."

"Really," Jazz echoed. She and Kim had walked over to where the three girls were standing by Breezy's locker.

Crystal just nodded, secretly pleased at Breezy's total change of heart. She had known that all she had had to do was get Breezy to see why ballet was important. And Breezy clearly understood now. That thought made Crystal feel good.

"You don't have ballet today, do you, Crystal?" Jazz asked in concern, her blue eyes wide.

"No," said Crystal. "Not till tomorrow."

"And we *know* you don't have baseball practice," Terry added.

"And, unless I'm wrong, there's no major project due tomorrow, or test you have to study for, right?" Kim asked with a grin.

"Right," said Crystal.

"Well," Breezy said, "that settles it then. We're going to the Neptune in honor of the only ballet/baseball star in the history of professional sports. You've heard of baseball/football heroes like Bo Jackson. Well, Crystal Joseph brings new meaning to the term, 'multi-sport professional.' "

Crystal giggled. "Thanks," she finally replied. "You guys are the best."

"I know, I know," replied Breezy. "I'm glad that you're aware that you're dealing with greatness here —"

"Breezy," Kim interrupted, "your head is getting so big that there's not going to be enough room in this hallway for all of us if you don't shut up soon."

"Kim, where is your sense of humor?" Breezy kidded her best friend. "You obviously left it at home."

"I wouldn't talk, Hawk," Kim countered, her brown eyes twinkling.

"So, let's cruise," Jazz cut in. "I'm really psyched for one of Eddie's incredible ice cream concoctions."

When the girls got to the Neptune, the first thing they noticed was that Lindsay, Gwen, Beth, and Molly were there too. They were sitting at their usual table near the window. Lindsay always insisted on sitting near the window so she could see people who were coming into the diner before they walked inside.

"Come on," Jazz said to Crystal under her breath. "We're not going to let them ruin our celebration. Let's just pretend they're not even here."

Jazz slid into a booth, pulling Crystal in beside her. Breezy slid in next to Crystal, and Kim and Terry sat down on the opposite side of the table.

"Hey, gang," said Eddie, walking out from behind the counter and stuffing a rag into the belt of his white apron. "What's happening? You guys didn't have a game today, did you? Where's Ro?"

"No, Eddie," Jazz explained. "We didn't have a game today. We're here to celebrate something else."

Eddie's face brightened, and he looked around the table.

"So what's the celebration for?" he asked. "What's the good news?"

"Tell him, Crystal," said Kim.

"C.J. is going to be the Queen in this big-deal ballet," Breezy announced proudly.

"Princess, you mean," Jazz corrected her cousin. "Crystal is the lead."

"The lead, eh?" said Eddie, raising an eyebrow. "I'm impressed. I'd say that calls for something really special. Nifty Neon Surprise Sundaes all around."

In a matter of only a few minutes, Eddie was back at

their table with a tray filled with sundaes. Each sundae was a different color, with a second color of sauce on top. Crystal's was pink ice cream with bright red sauce topped with whipped cream and a cherry. Crystal shook her head in amazement. She didn't eat ice cream very often and when she did she usually just had a small dish of vanilla. She never, ever ordered sundaes.

"There," Eddie said, bowing. "I only hope that this humble snack is worthy of the star of the Hampstead Ballet Academy recital!" he concluded loudly.

"Well!" Lindsay exclaimed equally loudly, "I think it's really sad the way some people feel like they have to brag about any little thing, don't you, Gwen?"

Crystal sat up. She wasn't bragging. She couldn't help it if Eddie happened to have an incredibly loud voice.

"Gwen, you shouldn't feel bad at all," Lindsay continued in the same loud voice. "I mean, you know she only got the part because she's so *tall*. Anyway, it's not like it's really a professional performance. It's only a stupid part in a dinky recital."

"Really," Molly echoed. "It's no big deal!"

"Totally," Beth agreed. "Some people are just so rude!"

Breezy stood up and was about to open her mouth to yell at Lindsay and her gang, when Crystal grabbed her and pulled her back down into her seat. "It's okay, Breezy," Crystal said softly, staring seriously at her friend. "Really. They're just baiting us."

"But, C.J.," Breezy retorted, "we can't let those snobs get away with saying stuff like that about you."

"It doesn't matter," Crystal continued, calmly spooning up her sundae. "See, I know that Gwen really wanted my part and she feels bad she didn't get it. I don't want us to make her feel any worse. It's not fair to her."

Breezy stared at Crystal for a minute without saying a word. "Got it," she suddenly said with a smile. "All right, all right, we'll let them off easy this time, but next time . . . " she let her voice trail off and began to cackle evilly.

"Crystal's right. Forget about them," Terry said, taking a big bite of her green ice cream with chocolate sauce. "Those guys are major jerks."

"Well, thanks for wanting to stick up for me," Crystal said with a smile.

"No problem, C.J.," Breezy replied. "Hey, we're a team, and a team's got to stick together."

"So, when do you start rehearsing?" Jazz asked Crystal. "I mean, since you're the star and everything you probably have to rehearse a lot, right?"

"Yeah, I guess so," Crystal admitted slowly.

"What's a lot?" Kim asked.

Crystal looked at them. "Well, I'm not exactly sure," she said. "But I might have to miss a few baseball practices between now and the recital."

"Miss a few practices?!" Breezy practically exploded.

"Why?" Terry asked.

"Well, for rehearsals," Crystal explained slowly.

Breezy stared at her. "But you've been taking ballet since you've been on the Parrots, C.J. You never had to miss practice before!"

"I know," said Crystal. "But this is different. Madame is scheduling a lot of extra rehearsals for Nikolai and me since we have the biggest parts."

"So what about the team?" Breezy demanded. "What are the rest of us supposed to do, just put the whole season on hold?!"

"I can still make it to all the games," Crystal said. Then she paused and thought for a moment. "At least, I'm pretty sure I can."

"Oh, that's just great," Breezy sputtered. "Look, don't do us any favors!"

Crystal took a deep breath. Why was Breezy making this so difficult for her? She had thought Breezy was on her side.

"You don't understand," Crystal began, "this is really important —"

"And baseball isn't anymore?" Breezy cut her off. "People depend on you, you know. Missing the end of practice once is one thing, but you can't go missing whole practices all the time."

"But I didn't mean that baseball isn't important," Crystal said softly.

Breezy stood up, her dark eyes flashing. "Yeah?" she retorted. "Well, I don't think you know what you mean.

You know, I was beginning to think you were a real pro. I was beginning to think you were serious about the Parrots. And I was even beginning to think there might be something to all those baseball books you read." She took a deep breath. "I can't believe that you're letting the team down like this, C.J.! I just hope you're happy!"

With that, Breezy turned and stormed out the door of the diner. Crystal was left sitting at the table with Terry, Jazz, and Kim. No one said anything. Crystal looked down at the melting pink and red mush that used to be her sundae and felt as if everything inside her was melting. She bit her lip so she wouldn't cry.

"Don't mind Breezy," Jazz said gently. "You know how she gets about the team."

"Well, she does have a point," Terry commented matter-of-factly, wiping some chocolate sauce off her chin with a napkin. "I mean, if we're going to make it as a team, we have to act like a team."

"I always try to do the best I can," Crystal said quietly. "You know I do. It's just that ballet is also important to me. I mean, I've never been the star in a recital before. It's as if I suddenly found out I was supposed to pitch for the first time in a game. I would spend as much time as I could practicing pitching in order to be the best I could be when it came time for the game."

"That's definitely true," Kim agreed, her brown eyes warm with concern. "I see what you mean, Crystal. And I'm sure you'll be able to work it out."

"Yeah, C.J.," Jazz put in, "you always figure out a way."

"Good luck," Terry commented, standing up. "Hey, I've got to rock and roll."

After the four girls had walked out of the diner and Crystal had said good-bye to Jazz, Kim, and Terry, she walked slowly home, thinking about what Breezy had said. She couldn't stand the thought that she might really be letting the team down. But ballet was just as important to her, and the opportunity to dance the female lead opposite someone as talented as Nikolai might never come again. She wanted to be the Princess very much, of course. But what if it meant losing her spot on the team? She definitely didn't want that to happen, no matter what. The closer Crystal got to her house the more confused she felt. She really didn't know what to do.

8

Crystal leaned back against the wall of the ballet studio and watched Gwen lead the rest of the Fairies in a series of steps. Gwen seemed totally aware that the eyes of everyone in the room were on her as she stepped up onto one toe and balanced with one leg stretched behind her in an *arabesque.* Amelia, April, Leslie, and Allison fluttered around her. Coming down softly out of her *arabesque,* Gwen went into a series of *glissades* and *assemblés,* tiny and difficult jumps in which she beat her feet lightly against each other in the air before landing and springing into the air again. She did jump after jump quickly and perfectly. Crystal knew that Gwen was performing beautifully.

Crystal glanced nervously around the room. Everyone had been rehearsing really hard for the past few weeks, especially Nikolai and herself since they had the biggest parts. Today they were supposed to work on one of their most difficult dances. But Nikolai hadn't shown up. She could see that Madame was almost finished working with the Fairies. Crystal scuffed one of her pink ballet slippers against the floor, and began to wonder if she would have to work on her part alone.

Just then, Nikolai burst through the door, his dance bag slung casually over his shoulder. He was wearing a black tank top and a pair of snug gray sweatpants. Madame gave him a brief nod and went on supervising the Fairies.

Nikolai walked straight over to where Crystal was sitting, and flopped down next to her on the floor.

"Hello," he whispered, grinning.

"Hi," Crystal replied with a small smile.

Nikolai pulled off his sneakers and slipped on a pair of black leather ballet slippers. As he began stretching his muscles, he turned to Crystal again and smiled. Then he did something that surprised her even more — he winked.

Crystal had already warmed up, but she did a few more stretches just to make sure. If only she could get rid of the jumpy feeling in her stomach. Dancing with Nikolai made her incredibly nervous. She was sure he had really high expectations for his partner.

Just then, the Fairies' music ended and Madame tapped her stick against the floor.

"Very good, ladies," she announced to all the fairies. "You may have a seat now."

As Gwen walked past Crystal and Nikolai on her way across the studio, she turned her head the other way and acted as if she hadn't even seen them.

"All right," Madame continued, "now I will work with our Prince and Princess, please."

Crystal stood up shyly and followed Nikolai over to where Madame was perched on her high stool. Crystal knew that everyone in the room was looking at them, and she could feel her heart pounding. This was the first time they'd ever performed in front of the group.

Madame explained that they were going to work on the scene in which the spirit of the Princess appears to the Prince as he is hunting in the woods. She instructed Crystal to stand off-stage and wait for her entrance. Then she told Nikolai to dance the part where the Prince is supposed to be hunting in the woods.

As Crystal took her place, the music began and Nikolai struck a pose. As the music got louder, he began to dance, and Crystal recognized the steps as the ones she had first seen Madame teaching him. Again Nikolai seemed to leap to the ceiling, and to hang in the air forever, before landing softly on his feet. Crystal was amazed. He was incredible — like a young Baryshnikov.

When Nikolai finished his solo, Madame instructed Crystal on her entrance as the spirit of the Princess who appears to the Prince in the woods. She remembered that this was the scene where the Prince and the Princess are supposed to fall in love. That thought only made Crystal even more nervous.

The music began again, and Crystal stepped lightly

on stage. She did her best to float around Nikolai the way the spirit of the Princess was supposed to, but she could feel her knees shaking.

Then they got to the part where the Prince was supposed to take the Princess's hand so they could begin their dance together. Crystal felt Nikolai take her hand in his. Shyly, she looked into his face as he led her across the floor. His eyes were such a deep shade of blue and sparkled so much, Crystal wondered why she hadn't noticed them before. She and Nikolai held each other's gaze as they danced the series of steps together. Crystal's knees felt weak and her heart was beating even faster than it had been before. All of a sudden, everything Jazz had ever said about having a crush on a guy filled her brain. Staring into Nikolai's blue-blue eyes, like the Princess in the ballet, Crystal felt herself falling in love with the Prince.

Finally, the music ended, and Crystal was startled when the room broke into applause. She had completely forgotten that there were other people there besides Nikolai and herself. She'd even forgotten about Madame. Looking around, now that the spell of their dance was broken, Crystal could see that the girls sitting around the edges of the studio were beaming. Only Gwen was looking off in the other direction as if she hadn't even noticed their dance.

Suddenly, Nikolai stepped directly in front of Crystal and bowed deeply from the waist.

"Very nice," Madame commented, getting up from her stool. "But now there are, of course, a few things that need work." She turned to the class. "The rest of you may go. These two will stay and work with me some more."

After the rest of the class had left the room, Madame explained to Crystal and Nikolai what they needed to improve. By the time they had finished rehearsing an hour and a half later, Crystal was exhausted.

"All right, this was good," said Madame. "You are learning. I will see you both back here Saturday morning." With that, she picked up her stick and walked out of the studio.

Crystal took a deep breath and wiped the sweat from her forehead. She didn't think she'd ever worked so hard to get something down perfectly — except in baseball when she was first learning how to bat.

"You like some?" Nikolai asked, offering Crystal the bottle of mineral water he'd taken out of his dance bag.

"Thanks," said Crystal, taking it from him.

"I notice you have not been wearing your special makeup," Nikolai commented with a grin.

Crystal wondered what he was talking about for a minute until she remembered what had happened a few weeks ago with the eye-black. "Yeah," she replied, as she felt herself blushing.

"What is it for really, this face paint you wore?" Nikolai asked, a confused expression on his face. "It is American fashion?"

"No," Crystal explained with a smile, "it's eye-black. It prevents glare when you're playing baseball."

"Baseball?" Nikolai repeated, still confused.

"You know," said Crystal, as she pretended to lift a bat over her shoulder and swing.

"Ah, yes," Nikolai said, his face brightening. "This I have seen. But you do this baseball?"

"Sure," said Crystal. "It's fun."

"Fun? Yes?" asked Nikolai. "But in my country it would not be permitted for dancer to do this."

"Really?" Crystal asked, her forehead wrinkled in surprise. "Why not?"

"In my country," Nikolai explained, "a dancer must dedicate his life to dancing. It is great privilege to be allowed to go to ballet school."

Crystal was amazed. "You mean, not just anyone can take ballet classes?"

Nikolai slipped out of his ballet slippers and shook his head. "No," he said. "In Soviet Union, ballet school is run by government. Only most talented students are allowed to study. My parents brought me to the ballet school when I was very young. They were very happy when I was accepted, although they have missed me."

"Missed you?" asked Crystal. "Didn't you live with them?"

"In Soviet Union, ballet students live at school," Nikolai told her, lacing up his sneakers. "Like American boarding school. Except we study mostly dancing. Only a little about other subjects — and no baseball," he added with a grin.

Crystal was amazed. She wondered what she would do if she had to choose between ballet and living at home with her family. She wasn't sure that she'd be willing to give up playing baseball and doing all the other things she loved.

"I would like very much to talk more to you about our countries," Nikolai was saying. "I have much to learn if I will be staying in United States. Perhaps we could go out together on Saturday after rehearsal — to talk more."

"Um, well, maybe," Crystal stammered in surprise.

Nikolai threw his dance bag over his shoulder and grinned. "Good-bye!" he said, heading toward the door. "Until Saturday!"

Crystal hurried back to the dressing room, her mind buzzing. She couldn't believe that Nikolai had just asked her out. She also couldn't get over what he had been telling her about studying ballet in Russia. He was so dedicated to dance. It really made her think about how different things were in the United States.

As Crystal slipped her gray sweatshirt over her head, a terrible thought suddenly struck her. Nikolai was 15 years old, and Crystal was only 12 and she had never been out on a date in her life. Was it okay for the two of them to go out? Was it really a date? As she laced up her sneakers, she decided that since they were dancing the leads in a major ballet production together and since they were going out to discuss ballet, then it was different than a regular date. So it was okay.

On her way home, Crystal started getting more and more excited. Nikolai was so talented and so dedicated to ballet. She could probably learn a lot from talking to him. And it didn't hurt that he also happened to be pretty good-looking. Crystal had never really thought about boys like that before, but when he had gazed at her with those incredibly piercing blue eyes of his . . . well, Crystal's heart had started beating like crazy. According to what Jazz always said about crushes, that was a sure sign. Crystal smiled as she turned up her driveway. She couldn't wait until Saturday.

9

"Now we begin right away," Madame said brusquely on Saturday morning, as she tapped her stick sharply against the floor. "We have only five days to go. Our dress rehearsal is on Thursday. There is much work to be done. We start with the Lilac Fairy."

Crystal didn't know how she had gotten through the past two days. She had been so nervous and excited about this rehearsal and about going out afterward with Nikolai. She knew Breezy was still mad at her, but she didn't know what to do about it. Breezy just didn't understand why this recital was so important. Crystal hadn't even told her about Nikolai and their "date," or whatever it was. In her entire ballet career, Crystal didn't think she'd ever been so excited about dancing before. Nikolai was definitely a great influence for everybody with his incredible talent and dedication. He made the world of dance seem so glamorous and important.

Crystal saw Gwen stand up and walk to the center of the floor.

"I wish to do the scene where the Lilac Fairy comes to the Prince in the woods and leads him to the Sleeping Beauty," Madame continued.

Nikolai and Crystal both stood at the mention of their parts.

"We will not need you for this scene, Miss Joseph," Madame said, turning to Crystal.

Crystal felt herself blushing as she sat back down on the floor. She couldn't help but notice Gwen smirking in her direction. Then she saw her smile sweetly at Nikolai as she walked over to him.

"For now we use our imaginations, and the Princess lies there asleep, waiting for the Prince," Madame said, pointing with her stick toward a folding table on one side of the room. "In this scene, the Princess only sleeps. And, since I am certain that Miss Joseph has plenty of opportunity to practice sleeping at home in her own bed, we will not ask her to practice that here now."

Crystal heard some of the girls giggle, and wondered why she suddenly felt so self-conscious.

As usual, Nikolai's dancing was amazing to watch. The room was completely quiet as he went through a series of six enormous *assemblés,* kicking one leg practically up to his ear and then somehow bringing both legs together, feet pointed, before landing without a sound. Then, leaping and springing with incredible speed, he performed a series of barrel turns across the floor, finally jumping into the air for a *tour jêté* turning his body completely around, and finishing in a pose on one knee.

That was Gwen's cue to enter. With her arms crossed demurely in front of her, she danced across the floor, balanced perfectly on her toes, taking steps so tiny she seemed to be floating. When she reached Nikolai, she stepped softly off her toes and tilted her head toward him elegantly before beginning the graceful series of arm movements and body poses that were supposed to tell the story of *The Sleeping Beauty*. As Gwen danced her way around Nikolai, Crystal couldn't help noticing that their eyes never left each other. She wondered if that was how she and Nikolai looked when they danced together. She had thought that was only supposed to happen between the Prince and the Princess.

After Gwen and Nikolai had finished, Crystal leaned forward to stretch her legs. She and Nikolai were supposed to learn the wedding scene next and she wondered where he had wandered off to. Besides, they hadn't decided where they were going to go after rehearsal. She was thinking of suggesting the Neptune.

Just then, she noticed Nikolai on the other side of the room talking and laughing with Gwen. Crystal felt her hands ball into fists at her sides. She couldn't believe herself — she was jealous! This was another sign of having a crush, according to Jazz. But she reassured herself that Nikolai was probably just talking to Gwen about the scene they had done together.

"Now I must work with my Prince and Princess,"

Madame announced, rapping her stick for attention. "We have much work to do. The rest of you may go."

Crystal walked slowly to the center of the room. She stood waiting for Nikolai to join her, but he was still talking to Gwen. "Bye-bye, then!" he called out to Gwen, as he began walking toward Crystal. "I see you later!"

Crystal frowned in confusion. What did Nikolai mean by telling Gwen he would see her later? The two of them were supposed to go out and talk about ballet. Maybe he meant that he'd see her at practice on Monday.

Madame proceeded to work Crystal and Nikolai as hard as usual, stopping them often to make corrections. By the time they were finished, Crystal was hot and tired, but she felt satisfied. She could tell without being told that the two of them were dancing well together. It had been hard juggling ballet and baseball, but Crystal had been trying her best. In fact, the Parrots had won their game against Tony's Pizzeria the weekend before — but only by a breath. Crystal felt bad about missing some practice time in between, but she thought she was managing her time pretty well. Her baseball was really only suffering a *little* bit.

"Nikolai," Crystal began, turning shyly to face Nikolai as soon as Madame had left the room, "do you know where you want to go?"

"Go?" he asked, looking up at her with a puzzled expression on his face as he pulled on one of his sneakers.

"After class," Crystal replied shyly. "Don't you

remember that you asked me to go out?"

"Oh, yes," Nikolai said, brightening. "Very good then. It will be like party."

"Yes, I guess," Crystal said, wondering what he meant by a party, but shrugging it off as just a confusion in language. "I'll go change and meet you outside."

"Okay," replied Nikolai, flashing her one of his most brilliant smiles.

Crystal changed as quickly as possible. She gave herself one quick look in the mirror. She was wearing a pair of olive-green suspender pants and an off-white T-shirt with a matching olive-green cropped jacket and off-white socks. She hoped she didn't look too color-coordinated, but Jazz always told her that she looked like a model in this outfit.

By the time Crystal got outside, Nikolai was already waiting. He told her he wanted to go to the pizza place around the corner. Crystal thought that was fine, so she didn't bother suggesting the Neptune. Anyway, there would probably be people at the diner who knew her. This way, they could have some privacy. Crystal smiled at the thought of being alone with Nikolai. It made her feel excited and nervous at the same time.

As the two of them walked around the corner, Nikolai reached over and linked his arm through Crystal's. This made Crystal's stomach flutter even more. It was her first date, after all, even if it was only going out for pizza at two o'clock in the afternoon. And she'd never gone out alone like this with a boy before.

Nikolai pulled open the door to the Pizza Palace and stepped inside, with Crystal close behind him. They stood there for a moment in the doorway as Nikolai looked around the room. Crystal wondered what he was waiting for since there were plenty of empty tables. All of a sudden, he grabbed her hand and pulled her over to a table in the corner. Crystal almost fainted when she saw who was sitting there: Gwen and Lindsay!

"Hello!" Nikolai said, smiling broadly at them and pulling out a chair.

Crystal just stood there in shock. She couldn't believe this was happening. Her first date ever — and Gwen and Lindsay were there!

"What are *you* doing here, Crystal?" Gwen asked, glaring at Crystal.

"What am *I* doing here?" Crystal echoed. "What are *you* doing here?"

"Nikolai invited me," Gwen explained huffily, flipping her auburn curls over her shoulder.

"Well, Nikolai invited me, too," Crystal retorted, her brown eyes blazing.

"He did?" Lindsay added in her most obnoxious voice.

"Is wonderful, no?" Nikolai asked. "We can make a party together, yes?" Before any of the girls could say anything, he continued. "This is best friend I was to meet?" he asked Gwen, looking intently at Lindsay.

"I'm Lindsay Cunningham," Lindsay announced with a sickly sweet smile and a toss of her white-blonde hair. "It's so nice to meet you, Nikolai."

"Sit down, Crystal, sit down," Nikolai said, turning to Crystal all of a sudden as if he had just remembered she was there, and pulling out a chair for her.

Crystal didn't know what to do, so she just sat down numbly.

"This is fun, yes?" Nikolai continued, looking around the table. "I hope to have many girlfriends in America."

Crystal wondered if Nikolai had learned enough English to know the difference between a friend who was a girl and a girlfriend.

"Ooooh," Lindsay exclaimed with a giggle. "I just love your accent, Nikolai."

"Yes, really?" he asked, tilting his head down and looking up at Lindsay through his eyelashes. "I am afraid it sounds ugly."

"Oh, no," Gwen gushed. "Not at all."

Nikolai smiled happily. As she sat there watching the three of them, Crystal got the definite feeling that Nikolai was enjoying all of the attention — a lot.

"I am thinking," he said, suddenly serious, "that my name, Nikolai, is maybe not good for one who will be living in America."

"Oh, no!" exclaimed Gwen, staring at Nikolai in concern.

"But it's such a great name," Lindsay added.

"Yes," Nikolai said. "You think? Is there not some name more American — I have heard it said, but I do not know it now — something that is almost the same as Nikolai?"

"Oh!" Lindsay squealed, "I know! You mean Nick. You know, like a nickname for Nicholas?"

"Yes," Nikolai said. "This I like — Nick. It has a strong sound, no?"

"Oh, very," Gwen breathed, batting her eyelashes at Nikolai.

Nikolai grinned. "From now on, I am Nick!" he announced, flexing an arm muscle. "Nick! You like?"

"Oh, yes," Lindsay and Gwen answered together. "We like." Then they both giggled, staring at Nikolai as if he was the most incredible thing they had ever seen.

Crystal shifted uncomfortably in her chair. She was beginning to think she liked the new Nick a lot less than she had liked the old Nikolai. One thing was for sure, this "date" certainly wasn't turning out anything like she had expected. She couldn't believe the way Lindsay and Gwen were falling all over Nikolai. And Nikolai seemed to be loving every second of it.

"So, do you girls play the baseball with Crystal?" Nikolai asked. Crystal looked down at her feet, wishing she could somehow make herself disappear.

"Oh, no!" Lindsay answered quickly, looking horrified.

"Where did you *ever* get that idea, Nick?" Gwen

asked, shooting Crystal a snide look.

"Most American girls hardly *ever* play rough sports like that," Lindsay said. "At least not the ones *you* would want to meet."

Before Crystal could say anything, the waitress came over to take their order.

"Excuse me," Crystal said, standing up and pushing back her chair, "but I really have to leave now."

"Yes?" Nikolai asked, looking up at her. Then he smiled, shrugged his shoulders, and turned to Gwen and Lindsay. They were both leaning so far toward him across the small table that they looked as if they were about to tip it over. "So," Nikolai continued, "is okay, no? We three make party together then."

Crystal turned and walked toward the door. She could hear Gwen and Lindsay giggling, but she didn't care. Nikolai was such a phony. He was nothing like what Crystal had thought he was. And she didn't have a crush on him anymore — that was for sure.

10

On Thursday afternoon, Crystal watched Ro pace back and forth in the dugout. Ro always paced before games. And Dudley's was going to be a tough team to beat. It was also the day of the dress rehearsal, and Crystal was really nervous. They'd been rehearsing every day, but Crystal still didn't feel as if she was prepared.

Sitting on the bench between Jazz and Terry, Crystal shot another look at Breezy. Breezy was staring straight ahead at the field, though, and wouldn't meet her eyes. Crystal's stomach felt as if it was tied up in knots. And it wasn't just because of the game.

Ever since Breezy had stormed out of the diner, Crystal had been trying to figure out how to explain things to her. It didn't help matters that Crystal had had to miss practice entirely on Tuesday to go to ballet for a costume fitting. Or that they'd almost lost that game the week before.

The part of the Princess was demanding and Crystal

knew that she had never ever worked so hard in ballet. Luckily, the dress rehearsal was after the game, but Crystal was really going to have to rush to Madame's in order to make it there in time.

Why couldn't Breezy understand, Crystal wondered. It wasn't as if rehearsals for *The Sleeping Beauty* were going to last all season. They were almost over. Crystal couldn't control when Madame scheduled costume fittings and rehearsals. But she knew that Breezy still thought that she was letting the Parrots down. That made Crystal feel terrible because she worried that it might be true.

Crystal turned to face Ro again. The coach walked back and forth, snapping her gum. Ro was wearing a black and white long-sleeved polka-dotted shirt and black and white biker shorts under her Pink Parrots jersey. Even her long nails were polished in black and white and had little checks all over them.

"There's Jimmy Hsu. The guy who hit three home runs," Terry announced suddenly, gesturing to a short, stocky boy with a black crew cut.

"I thought he'd be a lot bigger," Jazz commented.

Terry laughed. "What does that have to do with anything?" she asked.

"Well, if he could hit all those home runs, he should be big," Jazz replied and then turned to Crystal. "Don't you think so?"

"It doesn't really matter how big he is," Terry

answered. "All that matters is that he hit three home runs in a single game."

"Okay, birds!" Ro called out, interrupting them. "Let's get together here. We're up first. That's Breezy, Crystal, Kim. Relax and visualize so we can get some early numbers up, okay?"

Crystal watched Breezy pick up her bat and slide a weighted donut on it. Breezy headed out to the on-deck circle without saying a word. She started swinging her bat around to loosen up.

"Look, Andy Garcia's pitching," Terry remarked as Dudley's took the field. She pointed at a tall, dark, curly-haired boy climbing onto the pitcher's mound.

"Is he good?" Crystal asked, looking for her bat.

"Didn't you go over everyone's stats last night like you usually do?" Terry asked, surprised.

Crystal shook her head. "I didn't have time," she admitted. "I had a rehearsal and then I had to finish my lab report."

"I can't believe it," Terry continued. "You always know all about everyone."

Crystal had felt bad enough climbing into bed the night before with the stack of Dudley's stats unread. But now she felt worse. The team counted on her information. And sometimes it could make the difference between winning and losing.

"Come on, Breezy!" Kim called from the bench as Breezy stepped into the batter's box. "Get a dinger!"

Crystal watched as Breezy crouched into her low batting stance and Andy went into his windup. The ball thumped into the catcher's mitt as Breezy took the first pitch for a strike.

Next, Andy shot a fastball toward home plate. The ball never reached the catcher. Breezy caught a piece of it and blooped the ball into shallow rightfield. She held up on first for a single.

Crystal headed up to the plate, her bat dragging behind her. She felt totally unprepared for this game. Her mind had been so focused on ballet lately that she had a hard time remembering how to hold the bat. She wished again that she had gone over Dudley's stats the night before — at least, Andy Garcia's. She didn't even know what kind of pitch he liked to throw most often or his strikes-to-pitches ratio, or anything.

Digging her right cleat in the dirt, Crystal faced Andy and waited for the pitch. The first one came in low, so Crystal took it for a ball.

"A walk's as good as a hit!" Ro screamed from the dugout. Crystal swung her bat a few times and then dug in again. She noticed that Andy had a tendency to roll his eyes back as he went into his windup. The next thing she knew, the ball was headed right for her.

Swinging wildly, Crystal scooped the ball and popped it foul.

Determined to get a hit, Crystal really bore down on the next pitch. Unfortunately, she had been expecting a fastball. Andy threw a beautiful change-up instead. With her timing messed up, the best Crystal could hope for was another foul.

Glancing at first base, Crystal tried to catch Breezy's eye. It was weird to be up at bat and not hear Breezy cheering for her. Crystal was sorry that she had missed practice, but she was here at the game, wasn't she? And she could really use some support right about now.

"Let's go, Crystal!" Jazz screamed from the dugout as if she had read Crystal's mind.

Checking her swing just in time, Crystal took the fourth pitch for a ball. The count was now two balls, two strikes.

She stepped out of the batter's box and took a deep breath. Hitting was such a mental thing. Crystal felt guilty that her head wasn't all there. Part of her was thinking about her opening combination in *The Sleeping Beauty* instead of focusing on the game. Crystal shook her head to clear it and looked at the bat in her hand. She had to keep reminding herself that she was on the field to play baseball — not dance.

She stepped back up to the plate. If Crystal could get a hit, Breezy would see that she was really trying. And then she wouldn't be mad anymore. She would see that Crystal could still give her all to baseball even if she had missed some practice time and hadn't read the stats.

Andy went into his windup and delivered. Crystal jumped back to get out of the way. The pitch was way inside. Now the count was full, three balls and two strikes.

"A walk's as good as a hit!" Ro screamed again from the dugout.

Crystal definitely agreed with that — usually. But now, a hit would most certainly be better. It would really show Breezy that Crystal was not about to let the team down, not when it really mattered.

Gripping her bat, Crystal faced Andy and waited for his final pitch. She concentrated on the ball coming toward her and swung as hard as she could. But she never even made contact. The ball had been much lower than she had thought. In fact, it wouldn't even have been a strike if she hadn't swung. Crystal dropped her head in disappointment. How could she have swung at such a bad pitch with a full count? It went against everything she had ever read about batting.

Walking out of the batter's box toward the dugout, Crystal yanked off her batting helmet in disgust. She had been so anxious to prove to Breezy that she wasn't going to let the team down that she had done just that. She had struck out.

"Don't worry about it, Crystal," Jazz said as Crystal sat down next to her. "It happens to me all the time."

"It won't anymore," Terry interrupted. "Especially since we had that extra long practice concentrating on hitting on Tuesday."

"You guys had a hitting practice?" Crystal asked. It

was obvious that she really could have used some batting practice. And where had she been? Getting fitted for her costume. It was pretty clear to her that she had let her team down. Then again, it was still only the first inning. Crystal was determined to outplay everyone else for the rest of the game. That was all there was to it.

"All right, Kim!" Terry screamed, jumping up.

Crystal looked at the field in time to see Kim sprinting for first. The leftfielder was scrambling for the ball.

Breezy held up at second, as Kim overran first.

"Okay, Parrots!" Terry yelled, stalking out to the plate. "I'm going to send you all home."

Terry, a lefthanded hitter, dug her left cleat in viciously. Crystal noticed that Andy seemed unaffected by Terry's monster look. Crystal thought it was intimidating. She couldn't imagine why Andy didn't think so.

Terry swung hard at Andy's first pitch. Like Crystal, she looked as if she had been caught unaware by the change-up. But she powered a hit that seemed headed for home run territory.

"Way to go, Terry!" Breezy yelled from second.

The ball kept rising and rising. Crystal thought for sure that it was long gone. Dudley's centerfielder ran out to the wall and stretched way up. He leapt at the moment the ball was just about to clear the fence and fall to the ground. Everyone held their breath until the centerfielder raised his glove aloft — with the ball in it.

Terry flipped her bat and headed back to the dugout.

Even Jazz, Terry's closest friend on the team, knew enough to leave her alone for a few minutes. Terry plopped down at the end of the bench.

Now there are two outs, Crystal thought. She hoped that Sarah would be able to get on base. It would be terrible to leave two Parrots stranded out there, unable to score.

Sarah, unfortunately, hit the ball right to the shortstop. He flipped it to the second baseman. And that was that. Three outs. The Parrots were retired without scoring in their half of the inning.

Grabbing her glove, Crystal headed out to first base. They had five and a half innings to go, Crystal kept repeating to herself. It wasn't as if they were losing or anything. Besides, Crystal knew very well that baseball was all about the unexpected.

Breezy got the leadoff man in four pitches. Mark Wilson, the second batter, popped up right to Kim.

Two outs. Crystal took a deep breath to calm herself. See, she told herself. The Parrots were still playing well. A half inning didn't mean anything.

Johnny Wolfson was up next. Swinging at Breezy's first pitch, he blooped the ball right over Crystal's head. Crystal sprinted back a few steps and scooped up the ball. Without looking around, she pivoted and leaped for first base. She *had* to get this guy out. Especially after striking out before.

Suddenly, Crystal crashed right into Breezy — hard.

Crystal fell to the ground. She looked over toward Breezy. The pitcher was sprawled on the dirt a few feet away.

"Safe!" the umpire yelled.

"What were you doing?!" Breezy asked, obviously trying to keep from screaming. "Where is your mind?"

Crystal looked wordlessly at Breezy. Her mind *was* on the game. Why did it seem that the harder she tried to show Breezy that, the worse things got?

"You know that I cover the bag when you're fielding," Breezy continued, standing up and brushing herself off. She looked down at Crystal. "Pay attention to what's going on, okay? I'm sure it's hard with all those tutus leaping around in your head, but try. Please."

With that, Breezy turned and stalked back to the pitcher's mound. Crystal sat there in the dirt for a moment. She knew she was trying too hard, but she couldn't seem to stop herself.

Picking herself up slowly, Crystal pushed her glove down farther on her hand and watched as Jimmy Hsu stepped up to the plate.

"Hey, did you hear about Jimmy's three home runs?" Johnny asked, grinning at Crystal. "All in one game."

"We heard about them," Crystal replied, and then wanted to kick herself. She never responded to any of the runners' goading — ever. By replying to Johnny's comment, she had broken one of her rules. Breezy was right, Crystal had to get her mind on the game.

Breezy shook off Terry's signal twice. Finally, they agreed and Breezy went into her windup.

Jimmy didn't hesitate. He walloped the pitch to deep leftfield.

Dudley's bench exploded with cheers as Jimmy held up at third and Johnny crossed home plate. Dudley's was up, 1-0.

Luckily, Breezy got Sean O'Brien to pop up behind the plate. Terry got under it and made the third out.

Crystal headed slowly for the dugout. No one said anything to her as she threw off her glove and sat down. She hoped she wouldn't have to bat this inning. She couldn't take it if she let her teammates down again.

The next few innings didn't go too well for the Parrots. By the top of the fifth, Dudley's Bar and Grill was beating the Parrots, 4-2.

Crystal led off the fifth inning. She jammed her batting helmet onto her head and stepped into the box. The Parrots were losing by two runs, and Crystal knew that one of those runs was her fault. She was determined to make it up by getting a hit now.

The first pitch was slightly low. Crystal didn't move. She wasn't going to make *that* mistake again.

Crystal concentrated as Joe Ramos, who had relieved Andy Garcia after the third inning, went right into his windup. The pitch looked as if it were headed right down the middle. Crystal made a careful note of its position before swinging and connected squarely with the ball.

Sprinting for first, Crystal scanned the field to find the ball. The ball had bounced into leftfield and was rolling along the foul line. As Crystal rounded first base, she felt her batting helmet fly off her head. Betsy, who was acting as first base coach this inning, was giving Crystal the hold-up signal. But she knew if she could turn this into a double she would help make up for her botched play in the first inning. She headed for second.

Out of the corner of her eye, Crystal spied the ball coming toward the second baseman. Without thinking, she dropped to her seat and went into a hook slide. Suddenly, she realized that she wasn't going to be able to stop as she made the tag. Digging the heel of her straight leg into the dirt, Crystal suddenly felt a twinge in her calf. But she could feel herself slowing. She might just make it.

Unfortunately, Crystal forgot to lay flat and slide under the tag. The second baseman tagged her shoulder and got her out by a mile.

Crystal stood up dejectedly without even bothering to dust herself off. Not only was she out, but her calf hurt. She must have strained a muscle during her slide.

Crystal went back to first, picked up her batting helmet, and headed toward the dugout, limping slightly. She couldn't believe it. She had been trying so hard to help the Parrots get ahead, but all she had done was let them down again.

Then things went from bad to worse. Kim struck out

and even though Terry got a single, it didn't help. Terry was stranded when Sarah hit a shot right back at the pitcher. Three outs. And they only had one more chance at bat.

In the bottom of the fifth, with Julie pitching, Dudley's scored another run on a homer by Jimmy Hsu. The score was 5-2 in Dudley's favor. And the Parrots couldn't get anything going in the sixth. Jazz, Julie, and Andrea were out, one-two-three.

Crystal felt awful. She looked over at Breezy, who was sitting at the far end of the bench, staring straight ahead of her with her arms crossed over her chest.

Crystal knew she had to leave right away for Madame's, but she couldn't stand the idea of leaving Breezy sitting there like that. She walked over to Breezy.

"Breezy —" Crystal began.

"Look, Crystal," Breezy cut her off. "I just can't talk to you right now, okay? Go to ballet rehearsal, or whatever. All right?"

Crystal opened her mouth to say something else, but thought better of it. Turning and walking away, she knew she was late for Madame's. But she didn't care. She didn't care if she missed the whole dress rehearsal if only she could make Breezy understand.

11

Jogging to Madame's, Crystal felt the strained muscle in her calf. It was really beginning to bother her. The best she could do was a sort of limping jog. Madame was going to be angry by the time she got to dress rehearsal. There was no way out of being late at this point.

As she hurried in the front door of the Academy, Crystal could hear the Fairies' music playing down the hall in the studio. The dress rehearsal had already started! Listening to the music, Crystal could tell that Nikolai's solo in the woods was about to begin. That meant she had less than five minutes to change into her costume and get into her place in time to float on stage as the spirit of the Princess.

Crystal hurried into the dressing room and tugged off her dirty uniform, leaving it lying in a heap on the floor. The Princess costume that she had gotten at the last rehearsal was hanging by itself on the rack against the wall. She tugged on the peach bodysuit and yanked the peach and white chiffon tunic over her head. Crystal jammed her feet into her toe shoes and laced them up her legs. Hurrying down the hall with her little silver crown in her hand and the white satin ribbons of the dress trailing behind her, Crystal knew her face must be grimy from the game. But there was no time to stop in the bathroom to clean up.

Crystal hurried into the studio, still pinning her crown to her hair. Madame turned her head and gave Crystal a look that said she was not pleased. Nikolai, dressed in black tights and his sparkling green Prince's tunic, was just finishing his solo. Crystal rushed to her place and got there barely in time to step out for her entrance.

Crystal did her best to float gracefully toward Nikolai, but she hadn't had any time to warm up. She could feel herself wobbling. To make matters worse, her calf muscle was really beginning to throb.

When the time came for Nikolai to take her hand, Crystal didn't even try to look into his eyes. He didn't like her anyway. He was just playing his part. She only hoped that she could get through the whole performance pretending to be in love with him. The one kind of person Crystal really disliked was a phony. And Nikolai was definitely that.

They performed their steps together, but Crystal knew she was not doing well. She was exhausted from the game — mentally and physically. Her feet didn't seem to be able to do what she wanted them to. Finally, their duet was over.

Then, it was time for the scene where the Lilac Fairy tells the Prince about the Sleeping Beauty. Crystal took her place on the folding table, which had been covered with a red velvet cloth to make it look like a royal bed, and lay down as if she were sleeping.

As Gwen made her entrance, Crystal peered out from under her eyelashes. As usual, Gwen was in perfect form as she fluttered around Nikolai. She's probably been here for hours warming up, thought Crystal. It just wasn't fair that she had had to come straight from the game like that.

What a terrible game it had been! Crystal started to relive all the worst moments — her bad play in the first inning, her strikeout, her failed double.

All of a sudden, she was aware of someone leaning over her. She opened her eyes and saw Nikolai's face. She had completely forgotten where she was. They were up to the part where the Prince kisses the Princess and wakes her from her sleep. Crystal held her breath, hoping that Nikolai wouldn't kiss her. That was all she needed. Luckily he didn't. He just bent over her for a moment so that it would look like a kiss to the audience.

Since he didn't kiss her, which was what she had wanted, Crystal didn't understand why she suddenly felt let down. Maybe it was because the reason why Crystal had loved the story of *The Sleeping Beauty* as a child was because she was enchanted with the love between the Prince and the Princess. But now she realized that playing the part didn't mean she would really fall in love. It was just acting. Nothing more.

Crystal knew that she was supposed to get up off the table and dance the wedding scene with Nikolai. She sat up slowly and tried to step down from the table. But for some reason, she couldn't get her right leg to move. Her calf! Her leg was totally stiff from lying there. What was she going to do? Nikolai was glaring at her, waiting for her to stand so they could begin their final duet. The music raced on ahead of them.

Finally, Crystal tugged at her leg with both hands to get it off the table. She managed to stand on it, but it hurt. She had no idea how she was going to get through the complicated steps of the wedding dance. But she knew she had no choice but to try. Madame was already upset with her. She would be even more angry if Crystal just stopped in the middle of everything.

She stepped up on her right toe and immediately fell back off it. Her calf was killing her, and there was no way she was going to be able to dance up on her toes like that. Crystal was going to have to try to do all the steps on flat feet. It was going to be very apparent that something was wrong with her, but she had no other option.

Crystal struggled to keep up with Nikolai. When she caught his eye, he glared furiously at her. It was obvious that he wasn't pleased with her performance — or at all curious about why she was performing so poorly. Crystal had to admit that she was doing a terrible job, but she wished Nikolai could have a little more patience. He had known from the beginning that he wasn't going to be dealing with an almost-famous Russian ballerina.

Crystal felt incredibly relieved when the duet was over and the rest of the dancers joined them for the finale.

Finally, the dress rehearsal ended. Madame rapped her stick sharply and called for attention.

"Please find a seat immediately," she said quickly. "We have much to talk about."

Crystal limped to the center of the room and found a spot in the back of the group. She hoped Madame wasn't too angry with her for her performance. She was sure her calf would be all right by the next day. It only felt like a strain. Thank goodness she hadn't pulled it or anything.

"I would like to remind you all," Madame began, "that the purpose of a dress rehearsal is to get a feeling for how the recital will be." She paused for a moment and looked around the room. "I found today's dress rehearsal to be very revealing."

"As you all know," she went on, "it takes a lot of dedication to be a great dancer — as I am sure Nikolai can tell you."

Crystal glanced over to where Nikolai was leaning against the mirror.

"It takes a great deal of dedication, and a great deal of time, especially if one has a leading role in a performance," Madame continued. Crystal shrunk down. She knew she hadn't exactly seemed like a dedicated dancer, showing up late like that and then messing up her part so badly. But she couldn't miss a baseball game — especially an important one.

"You cannot give half your energy to ballet and expect to be good," Madame continued, not letting up for a moment. Crystal knew that this lecture was meant just for her. "If you do not practice all the time, every day, your body will forget and get lazy. Ballet must be all-consuming. It is a full-time job. You cannot do it halfway."

"Also, everyone is depending on each other. If one person does not do a good job, it reflects badly on the whole company. What sticks in the mind of the audience is the one bad performance — not the fact that the rest of the company was superb."

Crystal wished the floor would open up and swallow her whole. She had let the whole Ballet Academy down. If she had performed like that during the actual recital . . . she shuddered. The whole Academy might have gotten a bad reputation.

"I am going to make a change now," Madame concluded. "This change is for the good of the recital. The role of the Princess will be danced by Gwen Billings. Gwen appears to have the time and energy that such a role requires. Crystal Joseph will take over as the Lilac Fairy."

Crystal just sat there, stunned. For a moment, she felt like she was going to cry. But then she realized that Madame might be right. It was obvious from the dress rehearsal that Crystal wasn't as dedicated to ballet as

Gwen. If she was, she would have left her baseball game and been at the Academy early to make sure she was properly warmed up.

But what was she going to tell her father? He was so proud that his little "Butterfly" was dancing the lead. And what about Breezy and the Parrots? She had let them down too. All in one day. All because she wouldn't choose between ballet and baseball. Now that she had disappointed the Parrots and the Sixth Division, what did she have left?

12

Later that night, Crystal lay in bed tossing and turning. It must have been after 11:00, but she couldn't seem to fall asleep. She didn't know how she was going to face Breezy and the rest of the Pink Parrots again, after letting them down so badly in the game.

Thinking about ballet, Crystal knew the other reason that she couldn't fall asleep. The recital was the next day and she still didn't know how to tell her father that the lead role had been taken away from her — basically because she played baseball, too. She knew that her father was going to be really disappointed.

After a few more minutes of kicking her blankets around, Crystal knew it was no use. She decided to go to the kitchen for a glass of milk. Walking down the stairs, she was surprised to see a light coming from the kitchen.

Arnie looked up as Crystal walked into the room. "What's up, Crys?" he asked in disbelief. "What are you doing awake?"

"I don't know," Crystal replied, shrugging. "I

couldn't sleep." She opened the refrigerator and pulled out the milk. "What are *you* doing?"

"Big exam tomorrow," Arnie said, pointing at all the books on the table. "Thought I'd try to do a little extra cramming. I'm almost ready to pack it in, though."

Crystal poured herself a glass of milk and sat down across from Arnie.

"So, what's got you up so late?" Arnie continued. "Is this, like, guy trouble or something?" he teased.

"Arnie, do you remember Mom?" Crystal asked seriously.

He put down his pencil. "Sure," he said. "Why?"

"Well, sometimes I think I can remember what she was like, but other times I think maybe I'm just remembering what she looks like in pictures and all that stuff that Dad says about her," Crystal said. "You know, how gentle and graceful and what a perfect lady she was." She paused and took a sip of milk, trying to figure out exactly what she wanted to say.

"Sometimes, I wish Dad wouldn't tell me that kind of stuff," Crystal continued. "It's like he's just trying to make me into her or something. She's a lot to live up to, you know? But I'm not her. I don't think I even really look like her."

"I don't know about that, Crys," Arnie replied after a moment of studying her face. "I think you look a lot like she did at your age."

"I do?" she asked in surprise.

"Definitely," Arnie said. "Didn't you ever see her picture in her junior high school yearbook?"

Crystal shook her head.

"Hang on a sec," Arnie continued, standing up. He walked over to the door that connected the kitchen to the garage and opened it. The Josephs had stacked all the boxes that hadn't been unpacked yet in the garage. "Don't go away. I know it's out here somewhere." He shut the door behind him.

Taking another sip of her milk, Crystal tried not to think about ballet — or baseball.

A few minutes later, Arnie came back into the kitchen carrying a dusty leather-bound book. He flipped through the pages and then handed it to Crystal.

She took the book from him and looked at the page in front of her. There in the lower right-hand corner was a picture of her mother, Loretta Foster, as her name had been back then. Crystal looked more closely. Arnie was right, the girl in the picture *did* look like her. The hairstyle was completely different, but Crystal's mother had the same smooth, light cocoa-colored skin, high cheekbones, and brown, almond-shaped eyes as Crystal.

"Wow!" Crystal exclaimed in surprise. "No wonder Dad's always saying I'm just like her. She must have been only a few years older than I am when he met her."

Arnie nodded.

"But that's just the problem," Crystal said, sighing and putting the book down. "I may look like she used to, but I'm not *like* her. Not really. And I'm not only Dad's little 'Butterfly' either. I like to do other things."

"What do you mean?" Arnie asked.

"I love baseball," Crystal said, keeping her fingers crossed, just hoping that she still had a team to play on. "I like playing with the Pink Parrots more than just about anything. I can't explain it. If I wake up in the morning and I know we have a game that day, I'm totally excited before I even get out of bed. Just putting on my uniform puts me in a good mood."

"I know what you mean," Arnie cut in, grinning. "That's how I feel when I'm catching a touchdown pass or after I've rushed for two hundred yards in one game."

"But the problem is that Dad really only wants me to do stuff that his little 'Butterfly' would do," Crystal continued. "You know, stuff that's feminine, like ballet."

"I thought you liked ballet," Arnie said, sounding confused.

"I do," she replied. "I like it a lot. But not enough to sacrifice everything for it, like you have to if you're going to be great. And I'm certainly not ready to give up baseball." Crystal paused for a moment and stared into her half-empty glass of milk. "And as a matter of fact, Madame pointed all of this out for me this afternoon when she took the lead in the ballet away from me and gave it to someone else."

"What?" Arnie asked, his eyes wide in shock. "Oh, no! That's terrible. No wonder you can't sleep."

"It's all right, Arnie," Crystal replied a little wearily. "It really is. I realized that the part Madame gave me instead is probably better for me anyway. I didn't have the time and dedication to perform a lead role in such an important recital. I mean, I didn't even warm up before rehearsal today. I was too busy playing baseball."

"If you say so," Arnie said, sounding only half-convinced.

"My only problem now is explaining the whole thing to Dad," Crystal went on. "Oh, and trying to figure out what I want to do, play baseball or dance. Because it seems like I can't do both."

"Did something happen at your game today?" Arnie asked after a minute as if he had suddenly realized that there was more to Crystal's problems than she'd told him so far.

"We lost. And it was all my fault," Crystal replied softly. "I missed some practice time because of rehearsals and my head wasn't exactly on the game today. I made some really stupid mistakes — mistakes I never should have made. I don't know if the Parrots will ever forgive me."

"Crys, it's only a game," Arnie said. "And I'm sure that the Parrots would never kick you off the team for one bad game. Hey, you used to be so levelheaded. What's going on?"

"I'm just really worried about Dad," Crystal said. "I don't know how he's going to take this."

"Take what?" Mr. Joseph suddenly asked from the kitchen doorway. "What are you two doing up?"

"Big chem test tomorrow," Arnie said, stacking up his books. "But I'm just about done. I think I'll hit the hay." He stood up and winked at Crystal, mouthing "good luck" to her.

After Arnie had walked out of the kitchen, Mr. Joseph sat down in his seat across from Crystal.

"What are you doing up so late, Butterfly?" he asked.

"I couldn't sleep," Crystal replied, trying to figure out how to broach the subject.

"I know, you're really excited about your recital, right?" Crystal's father said. "It's not every day that my Butterfly performs the lead in an important ballet with one of the Soviet Union's up and coming young dancers. There will probably be some pretty major newspapers there, right?"

"Why?" Crystal asked, confused. It was just the Hampstead Ballet Academy, after all.

"Well, to review this Russian guy," her father replied.

Crystal hadn't even thought of that. Her father was probably right. Silently she thanked Madame for giving the lead to Gwen. Crystal would have hated to be featured in every major newspaper in Maryland, maybe even the country.

"Uh, Dad, that's kind of why I couldn't sleep," Crystal began.

"It's understandable," he said, getting up to pour

himself a glass of milk. "Don't worry about it, though. Just go back to bed and try to sleep. You'll do great. You always do."

"Well . . . Dad . . . I have to talk to you about that," Crystal said, taking a deep breath. She paused for a moment and then went on. "Madame gave the lead to Gwen today. I'm dancing the role of the Lilac Fairy instead."

"What!?" Mr. Joseph exclaimed. "Why in the world did Madame do that?"

"I don't have the dedication for such a big part," Crystal replied, keeping her voice as even as she could. She had to make her father understand — now that she was finally beginning to understand herself.

"Is that what that woman told you?" he asked. "What was her real reason for doing this? I'm going to have to talk to her right away. I know we can straighten this out."

"No, Dad," Crystal said. "She was right. I *don't* have the dedication for it. I'm much happier dancing the Fairy part. Really."

"But, Crystal," her father began, shaking his head, "I don't understand. Ballet was always so important to you."

"It still is," she said. "But it's not the most important thing in the world. I really love playing baseball, Dad."

"Baseball?" he repeated, sounding confused. He took a sip of his milk, without saying anything else.

"Please don't be upset, Dad," Crystal pleaded. "I

know that Mom really loved ballet and everything, but I'm not her. I'm me. And I love baseball."

Mr. Joseph didn't say a thing for a long moment. Crystal fidgeted nervously in her chair.

"You know," he began thoughtfully, "I just assumed that you would naturally love the things your mother loved because you're her daughter and all. And you know that Loretta was really dedicated to ballet — at least until she met me."

"But, I *do* love ballet," Crystal cut in. "I just love baseball too."

"You're right, Butterfly. You're not your mother," her father went on after he'd thought over what Crystal had said for a few moments. "You're your own person. I guess I didn't even realize what I was doing. I'm sorry, honey. If you want to play baseball, then that's what you should do."

Crystal stood up and hugged her father. "I'll still take ballet, Dad," she said.

"You don't have to, honey," her father replied. "Not just to make me happy."

"I want to," Crystal insisted.

"Okay," Mr. Joseph said, hugging her back. "Now skedaddle to bed. It's getting really late and you need your rest. And don't worry about it — you're going to be a great Fairy."

"Thanks, Daddy," Crystal said, walking out of the kitchen. On her way upstairs, she felt relieved that one of her problems had been solved. So she didn't really have to choose between ballet and baseball — she could do them both. Now, she just had to make Breezy understand.

13

"Somebody tie my ribbon!" Gwen called out frantically. It was the night of the performance and everyone seemed to be incredibly nervous — except for Crystal. Now that she didn't have to dance the lead, she felt as if a great weight had been lifted from her shoulders.

"Has anyone seen my other ballet slipper?" Allison asked.

Every performance Crystal had ever been in was like a madhouse beforehand no matter how well prepared the dancers were. Everyone was completely frantic, running around trying to get ready. Anyone walking into a dressing room 10 minutes before the recital would never believe that the show would go without a hitch — and be on time.

Crystal pulled off her red T-shirt dress and stepped calmly into the pink tights, lavender leotard, and lavender chiffon skirt that was the costume for the Lilac Fairy. She stopped in front of the small mirror to adjust the wreath of lilacs on her head.

"Hi, Crystal," said two voices behind her in unison.

Crystal turned around and saw Amelia and April in their Fairy costumes.

"You look wonderful," said Amelia.

"Really," agreed April.

Crystal smiled. "Thanks. You both look great too."

"Listen," said Amelia, "we're really sorry that Madame took away your part like that."

"Yeah," said April, "we thought you were a great Princess.

"But we're also really glad you're going to be the Lilac Fairy," said Amelia.

"Really," April whispered. "We'd much rather have *you* lead us in the Dance of the Fairies than Gwen."

Crystal laughed. "I'm glad too," she said. "The best part is, my calf is much better, and I hardly feel nervous at all."

Just then, Madame stuck her head in the dressing room door. "We begin in five minutes," she said. "Places, everyone!"

Crystal filed out behind the others and into the auditorium. She took her place in the wings, glancing quickly into the audience. Peeking around the curtain, she caught sight of Arnie, Kyle, and her dad all sitting in the second row.

Suddenly, the lights were lowered. Crystal couldn't believe how calm she felt. When the music began, she stepped onto the stage followed by the rest of the Fairies.

Without even thinking about what she was doing, Crystal didn't miss a step. It was as if her feet had a mind of their own and needed no guidance from her. Crystal felt as if only seconds had passed when the Dance of the Fairies came to an end. Leading the Fairies off stage, Crystal could hear the loud applause behind her.

Nikolai's solo was next. Watching him, Crystal thought that it was easy to see why he had such a promising future. She held her breath every time he soared in the air. And soar he did. Without a doubt, he was an incredibly talented dancer — no matter what he might be like as a person. When he finished — all too soon — landing on one knee, the audience broke out into loud, sustained applause.

When Crystal, as the Lilac Fairy, danced with Nikolai she could feel herself performing perfectly, taking the tiny leaps and steps just as she was supposed to. Nikolai was partly responsible for this, Crystal had to admit, because he was such a great partner. Crystal felt almost as if his smooth technique was flowing into her, helping her perform even better.

Then it was time for Gwen's entrance as the spirit of the Princess. Nikolai and Gwen danced together as if they had been made for it.

Later, Crystal noticed that when Nikolai had to kiss Gwen, he didn't just pretend as he had in the dress rehearsal with her. But Crystal didn't care. She still felt really good about everything since she'd made her decision about ballet and baseball.

The rest of the performance went very smoothly, and as the finale wound down, the audience exploded with applause and cheering.

The lights came up and Crystal and the rest of the Fairies took their bows first. All of a sudden someone let out a piercing whistle. Crystal almost fell off the stage when she saw Breezy sitting in the back row with Terry, Kim, Jazz, and the rest of the Parrots. Breezy had obviously decided that it was okay that Crystal was a "multi-sport athlete." Breezy waved at Crystal when she caught her eye. Crystal smiled broadly. She knew she'd made the right decision.

After everyone's bows were over, the dancers rushed to the dressing rooms. Crystal took off her costume, hung it on the hanger, and scrubbed the makeup off her face. As she was walking out the door, she bumped right into Gwen.

Neither of them said anything for a moment. Then Crystal smiled. "Gwen, you were a great Princess," she said, congratulating her. "You danced beautifully."

Gwen paused for a moment, as if deciding whether or not to believe Crystal. Then, suddenly, she smiled back. "Thanks, Crystal," she said. "You were very good as the Lilac Fairy, too. See you upstairs."

Crystal nodded and raced up the stairs. The Academy was serving coffee and doughnuts after the performance. Crystal knew her father and brothers would still be there waiting for her. She hoped the Pink Parrots would be, too — especially Breezy.

Arnie and Kyle nearly crushed her in a big double bear-hug as soon as she walked into the room.

"You were great!" squealed Jazz, suddenly running over and throwing her arms around Crystal.

"I thought you were pretty cool, too," said Terry.

Mr. Joseph made his way through the crowded room to his daughter.

"That's my Butterfly!" he said, hugging Crystal so that her feet dangled a couple of inches off the floor.

In his hand was a box wrapped in pink paper and tied with lace and satin ribbons.

"Here," he said, holding the box out to Crystal, "you deserve it."

Crystal took the frilly-looking box from him. She wondered what in the world it could be. Pulling it open, Crystal almost dropped the entire box on the floor. There, in a nest of pink tissue paper, was a brand new baseball glove!

Crystal looked up at her father in amazement. "But Dad . . ." she began.

"Like I said," Mr. Joseph repeated with a big smile, "you're your own person. Your mother and I knew you were a star from the day you were born."

Just then, Breezy pushed her way over to Crystal. In her arms was an enormous bunch of flowers.

"Here, these are for you," she said, giving the flowers

to Crystal. "From the team. *Your* team."

Crystal felt as if she was going to cry. Blinking furiously, she smiled at Breezy. "Thanks," she said softly. "I'm sorry —"

"Don't worry about it," Breezy cut her off. "I overreacted. You know how I get at games."

"But I let everyone down," Crystal protested.

"No, you didn't," Breezy contradicted her. "You just had a bad game. That can happen to anyone — even if you go to *every* practice."

"But —" Crystal tried again.

"Just forget about it, C.J.," Breezy interrupted once more with a wave of her hand. "Besides, it's not a crime if you have something else to do. I mean, that ballet looks like it's really hard work. You have to practice a lot to get to be as good as you are, so I figure it must be important to you. But that doesn't mean you don't care about the team. I heard that you lost the lead to Gwen because of the Parrots. So obviously, baseball means a lot to you."

Crystal looked around at her friends and family. She couldn't remember when she had been so happy. All of a sudden she remembered the baseball glove in her hand and felt a tingle of excitement. She couldn't wait to try it out at the next Pink Parrots practice.

About the Author

B. B. Calhoun

B. B. Calhoun grew up in New York City and still lives in Manhattan with her husband, a painter. She was a teacher and sports instructor at a private school in New York City. This is Ms. Calhoun's fourth book.

Watch for

CHANGE-UP

Number 5 in **THE PINK PARROTS** *series!*

"Slide, Breezy! Slide!" Ro yelled as John Connely, Ten Pin Bowling's third baseman, whipped the ball toward home plate.

Kim Yardley didn't even breathe as she watched Breezy race down the third base line. Suddenly, everything seemed to be happening in slow motion as the sounds of the screaming crowd faded away. The ball was still moving through the air, less than 10 feet from John's hand. Breezy's face was frozen into a grimace of concentration, her hat was halfway off her head, and her steps seemed to keep time with the pounding of Kim's heart.

Inch by inch, the ball got closer to the catcher's waiting glove as Breezy got closer to home plate and to scoring the tying run. Then Breezy raised her arms, bent her knee, and slid to the ground in a perfect textbook hook slide. Kim closed her eyes. She couldn't stand to watch.

"Safe!" the umpire yelled. Kim sighed in relief and opened her eyes.

"What's the matter with Breezy?" Jazz Jaffe asked a moment later. "Why isn't she getting up?"

Breezy was lying on her back on top of home plate, holding her knee, and rocking back and forth in obvious pain.

Kim immediately charged out of the dugout and over

to Breezy's side. Breezy grabbed her best friend's hand tightly and asked, "What happened?" She spoke through clenched teeth as the Emergency Medical Technicians examined her knee.

"You must have twisted your knee or—" Kim began.

"No! The run! Did I score the run?" Breezy moaned.

"Oh . . . yeah. The game's all tied up. But Breezy—"

"Kim, you've gotta promise me that you'll win the game," Breezy cut in, her eyes glittering with determination in her pale face. "You're the captain while I'm gone."

"Don't worry about the game," Kim said, trying to cheer up her friend. "Just think, you get to ride in an ambulance and—"

"Promise!" Breezy demanded weakly.

Kim swallowed hard. "I promise."

Then Ro was pulling Kim away and the two EMTs were lifting Breezy onto a stretcher and into the back of an ambulance.

Biting her lip to keep from crying, Kim watched as the ambulance drove away. What am I supposed to do now, she thought to herself. How can *I* be the captain of a baseball team? I don't even know where to begin!